Jajah.

SMP interact

TWYFORD CE HIGH SCHOOL
TWYFORD CRESCENT
LONDON W3 9PP

Higher
transition
practice

for AQA, Edexcel and OCR two-tier GCSE mathematics

CAMBRIDGE
UNIVERSITY PRESS

The School Mathematics Project

Writing and editing for this edition John Ling, Paul Scruton, Susan Shilton, Heather West
SMP design and administration Melanie Bull, Pam Keetch, Nicky Lake, Cathy Syred, Ann White

The following people contributed to the original edition of SMP Interact for GCSE.

Benjamin Alldred	David Cassell	Spencer Instone	Susan Shilton
Juliette Baldwin	Ian Edney	Pamela Leon	Caroline Starkey
Simon Baxter	Stephen Feller	John Ling	Liz Stewart
Gill Beeney	Rosemary Flower	Carole Martin	Biff Vernon
Roger Beeney	John Gardiner	Lorna Mulhern	Jo Waddingham
Roger Bentote	Colin Goldsmith	Mary Pardoe	Nigel Webb
Sue Briggs	Bob Hartman	Paul Scruton	Heather West

CAMBRIDGE UNIVERSITY PRESS

Cambridge, New York, Melbourne, Madrid, Cape Town, Singapore, São Paulo, Delhi

Cambridge University Press
The Edinburgh Building, Cambridge CB2 8RU, UK

www.cambridge.org
Information on this title: www.cambridge.org/9780521690010

© The School Mathematics Project 2007

First published 2007

Printed in the United Kingdom at the University Press, Cambridge

A catalogue record for this publication is available from the British Library

ISBN 978-0-521-69001-0 paperback

Typesetting and technical illustrations by The School Mathematics Project
Photograph on page 57 by Paul Scruton
Cover design by Angela Ashton
Cover image by Jim Wehtje/Photodisc Green/Getty Images

Using this booklet

This booklet provides well graded exercises that will help build confidence with national curriculum level 6/7 topics at the start of a Higher tier GCSE course, for example among students who have not followed an 'extension' course in key stage 3. The exercises can be used for homework, consolidation work in class or revision. They follow the chapters and sections of the *Higher transition* students' book, so where that text is used for teaching, the planning of homework or extra practice is easy.

Even when some other teaching text is used, this booklet's varied and thorough material is ideal for extra practice. The section headings – set out in the detailed contents list on the next few pages – clearly describe the GCSE topics covered and can be related to all boards' linear and major modular specifications by using the cross-references that can be downloaded as Excel files from **www.smpmaths.org.uk**

It is sometimes appropriate to have a single practice exercise that covers two sections within a *Higher transition* chapter. Such sections are bracketed together in this booklet's contents list.

Sections in the students' book that do not have corresponding practice in this booklet are shown ghosted in the contents list.

To help users identify material that can be omitted by some students – or just dipped into for revision or to check competence – sections estimated to be at national curriculum level 6 (or in a few cases level 5) are marked as such in the contents list and as they occur in the booklet.

Marked with a red page edge at intervals through the booklet are sections of mixed practice on previous work; these are in corresponding positions to the reviews in the students' book.

 Questions to be done without a calculator are marked with this symbol.

Questions marked with a star are more challenging.

Answers to this booklet are downloadable from **www.smpmaths.org.uk** in PDF format.

Contents

continues >

1 Calculation and estimation

A Decimals and place value
level 5

1 What does the 3 represent in each of these numbers?

    (a) 3 120 000   **(b)** 1.36   **(c)** 732.6   **(d)** 0.931   **(e)** 42.073

2 Put each list of decimals in order, smallest first.

    (a) 3.4, 3.5, 3.42, 3.1   **(b)** 0.2, 0.08, 0.23, 0.12

    (c) 0.709, 0.079, 0.79, 0.07   **(d)** 0.16, 0.0016, 0.106, 0.016

3 Write the answer to each of these.

    (a) 5.7×10 **(b)** $12.7 \div 10$ **(c)** 5.68×100 **(d)** $348.2 \div 100$

    (e) 7.93×10 **(f)** 3.2×100 **(g)** 0.304×100 **(h)** $1.2 \div 10$

    (i) 5.68×1000 **(j)** $4.9 \div 1000$ **(k)** $8.02 \div 100$ **(l)** $0.53 \div 1000$

B Multiplying by a decimal
level 5

1 Work these out.

    (a) 60×0.2 **(b)** 4×0.06 **(c)** 50×0.07 **(d)** 60×0.5 **(e)** 200×0.7

    (f) 500×0.4 **(g)** 0.4×0.02 **(h)** 0.8×0.5 **(i)** 300×0.04 **(j)** 3000×0.3

2 Use the numbers from the loop to find
as many pairs as possible whose product is

    0.5   5   50   500
    0.4   4   40   0.04

> You can use the same number twice.

    (a) 20   **(b)** 2   **(c)** 0.2

    (d) 0.16   **(e)** 0.25

C Dividing by a decimal
level 6

1 Work these out.

    (a) $\dfrac{10}{0.2}$ **(b)** $\dfrac{2.5}{0.5}$ **(c)** $\dfrac{14}{0.7}$ **(d)** $\dfrac{3.5}{0.5}$ **(e)** $\dfrac{32}{0.08}$

    (f) $\dfrac{0.6}{0.03}$ **(g)** $\dfrac{8}{0.02}$ **(h)** $\dfrac{4.8}{0.8}$ **(i)** $\dfrac{2.5}{0.05}$ **(j)** $\dfrac{0.6}{0.04}$

2 Sort these divisions into pairs that give the same answer.

    $\dfrac{0.4}{0.08}$ $\dfrac{0.3}{0.6}$ $\dfrac{5}{0.1}$ $\dfrac{0.1}{0.2}$ $\dfrac{1.5}{0.03}$ $\dfrac{3}{0.6}$

3 Work these out.

(a) $\dfrac{0.64}{0.4}$ (b) $\dfrac{0.3}{0.5}$ (c) $\dfrac{0.14}{0.2}$ (d) $\dfrac{0.09}{0.3}$ (e) $\dfrac{7.5}{0.5}$

*4 Work out the missing number in each of these calculations.

(a) $\dfrac{\blacksquare}{0.3} = 20$ (b) $\dfrac{3.6}{\blacksquare} = 18$ (c) $\dfrac{\blacksquare}{0.04} = 100$ (d) $\dfrac{5}{\blacksquare} = 250$

D Rounding whole numbers   level 5
E Rounding decimals   level 6

1 Round

(a) 32 786 to the nearest thousand   (b) 1 088 720 to the nearest ten thousand

(c) 60 498 to the nearest hundred   (d) 85 317 078 to the nearest million

(e) 349 903 to the nearest thousand   (f) 60 542 087 to the nearest million

2 Round

(a) 2.6084 to 1 d.p.   (b) 0.7493 to 2 d.p.   (c) 0.042 79 to 3 d.p.

(d) 1.008 32 to 2 d.p.   (e) 6.804 512 to 3 d.p.   (f) 14.8958 to 2 d.p.

3 Do these on a calculator and round each answer to two decimal places.

(a) 0.576×2.094 (b) $10.64 \div 2.18$ (c) 23.27×0.426 (d) $2.369 \div 0.862$

(e) $21.34 \div 7.85$ (f) 0.159×3.741 (g) $107.6 \div 28.4$ (h) 0.615^2

F Rounding to one significant figure

1 Round these numbers to one significant figure.

(a) 48 753   (b) 7821   (c) 20 424   (d) 795   (e) 3 863 088

(f) 0.0731   (g) 0.8742   (h) 2.0875   (i) 0.004 532   (j) 0.0973

2 Estimate the answers to these by rounding the numbers to one significant figure.

(a) 38×31 (b) 77×59 (c) 282×42 (d) 578×19 (e) 242×86

3 Work out a rough estimate for each of these.

(a) 0.48×41 (b) 2.7×49 (c) 0.0582×32 (d) 0.784×0.39

(e) 312×0.386 (f) 0.88×28 (g) 67×3.25 (h) 0.182×721

4 Grapes cost £4.18 per kilogram.
Estimate the cost of 0.645 kg of grapes.

5 Mike bought 41.8 litres of petrol at 91.9p per litre.
Estimate the amount he spent on petrol.

G Rounding to two or more significant figures

1 Round these numbers to two significant figures.

   (a) 56 842   (b) 2349   (c) 30 684   (d) 4038   (e) 5 963 174

   (f) 14.73   (g) 3.916   (h) 7.985   (i) 0.005 215   (j) 0.080 42

2 Round these numbers to three significant figures

   (a) 241 622   (b) 10 395   (c) 8427   (d) 304 067   (e) 13 258 083

   (f) 0.015 323   (g) 0.809 632   (h) 0.5019   (i) 0.007 318 3   (j) 2.006 422

H Sensible accuracy

1 Write each of the numbers in bold to a sensible degree of accuracy.

   (a) Helen's height is **1.652** m.

   (b) At the time of the accident, Joshi's car was travelling at **28.6423** m.p.h.

   (c) The area of Pat's garden is **627.3852** m^2.

2 The population density of a region (measured in people per km^2) is
  calculated by dividing the population by the area.

  East Island has an area of 386.4 km^2 and a population of 3130.
  West Island has an area of 213.8 km^2 and a population of 1740.

  Calculate the population density of each island.
  Round each result to a sensible degree of accuracy.

I Mixed questions

1 Given that $13 \times 27 = 351$, write down the answers to these.

   (a) 1.3×2.7 (b) 0.13×2.7 (c) 1.3×2700 (d) $351 \div 27$

   (e) $35.1 \div 1.3$ (f) $351 \div 0.27$ (g) $3.51 \div 2.7$ (h) $35.1 \div 0.13$

2 Round 4 065 729 to

   (a) the nearest hundred thousand   (b) three significant figures

3 A rectangular piece of cloth measures 6.79 m by 1.85 m.

   (a) Estimate the area of the piece of cloth by rounding the measurements
      to one significant figure.

   (b) Is your estimate bigger or smaller than the actual area?
      Explain how you can tell.

   (c) Calculate the actual area, giving your answer to three significant figures.

2 Graphing changes over time

1 Here are three different shaped bowls.
They are filled with water at a steady rate.

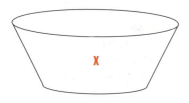 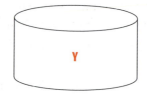 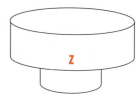

Match each graph below with a bowl.

(a) 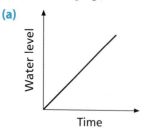   **(b)** 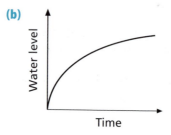   **(c)**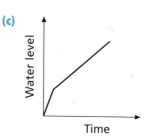

2 Look at these graphs.

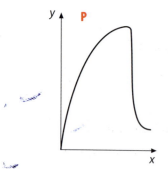 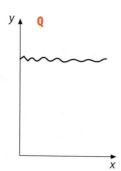 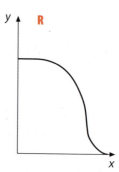 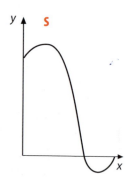

Each situation below matches one of the graphs above.

A   The height (*y*) above the water of someone diving from a diving board into
a pool, against time (*x*)

B   The speed (*y*) of someone sliding down a water chute, against time (*x*)

C   The temperature (*y*) in a heated swimming pool, against time (*x*)

(a)   Match each situation to its correct graph.

(b)   Suggest a situation for the unmatched graph.

3 Unitary method

A Problems

1 Here are the ingredients to make a spinach and mushroom omelette.

Spinach and mushroom omelette
Serves 2
4 eggs
200 g spinach
40 g butter
125 g mushrooms
10 ml mustard
140 ml soured cream
nutmeg and seasoning

  (a) How much spinach would you need to make a spinach and mushroom omelette for 6 people?

  (b) What weight of mushrooms would you need for 4 people?

  (c) How much butter would you need for 3 people?

  (d) How much soured cream would you need for 5 people?

2 Four identical tins of beans weigh 860 g altogether.
  What would be the weight of 3 of these tins of beans?

3 Five identical loaves of wholemeal bread cost £3.45 altogether.
  How much would I pay for 7 of these loaves?

B Cancelling common factors
C Using cancelling

1 Simplify each calculation by cancelling common factors and then evaluate it.

  (a) $\dfrac{17 \times 10}{2}$ (b) $\dfrac{21}{4} \times 12$ (c) $\dfrac{24 \times 33}{88}$ (d) $\dfrac{18}{42} \times 49$ (e) $35 \times \dfrac{27}{21}$

2 Mrs White buys 6 boxes of chocolates, each containing 20 chocolates.
  She wants to share out the chocolates equally among the 24 children in her class.

  (a) Which of these calculations gives the number of chocolates each child gets?

   $\dfrac{6 \times 24}{20}$ $\dfrac{6 \times 20}{24}$ $\dfrac{20 \times 24}{6}$

  (b) Simplify this calculation by cancelling.
      Work out how many chocolates each child gets.

3 Ten small sugar lumps weigh 18 g.
  What is the weight of 25 sugar lumps?

4 14 litres of water were collected from a dripping tap in 21 minutes.
  At this rate, how much water could be collected in 30 minutes?

5 (a) Jane's hair grows 12 mm in 30 days.
If it continues to grow at the same rate, how much will it grow in 40 days?

(b) When Jane had her hair trimmed, the hairdresser snipped off 18 mm of hair.
How long will it take for her hair to grow back to its original length?

D Using a calculator

1 Mr Jones travelled 182 miles on 23.6 litres of petrol.
The petrol tank in his car holds 55 litres.
How many miles, to the nearest mile, would Mr Jones expect to travel
on a full tank of petrol?

2 The table shows the amount of
carbohydrate and fat in 100 g of
different chocolate bars.

	Carbohydrate	Fat
100 g of Soft Centre	61.3 g	24.3 g
100 g of Chocolate Crisp	55.9 g	30.1 g

A Soft Centre bar weighs 16.7 g and a Chocolate Crisp weighs 21.9 g.

(a) Calculate the amount of carbohydrate in a Soft Centre bar.
Give your answer correct to the nearest 0.1 g.

(b) Which chocolate bar contains more fat and by how much?
Give your answer correct to the nearest 0.1 g.

3 (a) A piece of metal weighing 193 grams has a volume of 25 cm³.
What is the weight, to the nearest gram, of a similar piece of metal
that has a volume of 38 cm³.

(b) Another piece of the same metal weighs 124 g.
What is the volume, to the nearest cm³, of this piece of metal?

E Dealing with units of measure

1 One kilometre is equivalent to about 0.621 miles.
How many kilometres are equivalent to 27 miles?
Give your answer correct to two decimal places.

2 The exchange rate between euros (€) and US dollars ($) is €1 = $1.41.
(a) Change €48 into US dollars.
(b) Change $125.70 into euros. Give your answer correct to the nearest cent.

3 A certain set of scales measures in pounds (lb) and in kilograms.
A 14 lb bag is put on the scales and the scales show that it weighs 6.356 kg.
(a) What would be the weight in kilograms of a 20 lb bag?
(b) A small boy weighs 42 kg. What would be his weight in pounds?

4 Fractions

1 Copy these and find the missing numbers.

(a) $\frac{4}{5} = \frac{12}{}$ (b) $\frac{2}{7} = \frac{12}{}$ (c) $\frac{2}{9} = \frac{}{36}$ (d) $\frac{7}{8} = \frac{}{56}$ (e) $\frac{8}{11} = \frac{40}{}$

2 Write each of these fractions in its lowest terms.

(a) $\frac{24}{30}$ (b) $\frac{30}{45}$ (c) $\frac{14}{42}$ (d) $\frac{24}{40}$ (e) $\frac{32}{80}$

3 Change these mixed numbers into improper fractions.

(a) $3\frac{1}{4}$ (b) $2\frac{2}{3}$ (c) $3\frac{3}{4}$ (d) $2\frac{3}{8}$ (e) $1\frac{2}{5}$

4 Change these improper fractions into mixed numbers.

(a) $\frac{9}{2}$ (b) $\frac{11}{4}$ (c) $\frac{17}{5}$ (d) $\frac{17}{6}$ (e) $\frac{19}{3}$

5 In a typical working week, Aaron works for 35 hours.
He spends 5 hours on the phone, 14 hours meeting clients and
the rest of the time doing paperwork.

Write, in its simplest form, the fraction of the time Aaron spends

(a) on the phone   (b) meeting clients   (c) doing paperwork

6 Work these out.

(a) $\frac{3}{8}$ of 40   (b) $\frac{3}{5}$ of 40   (c) $\frac{5}{6}$ of 90   (d) $\frac{7}{8}$ of 72   (e) $\frac{5}{9}$ of 81

1 Work out which fraction in each pair is greater.

(a) $\frac{3}{4}, \frac{4}{5}$ (b) $\frac{4}{7}, \frac{15}{28}$ (c) $\frac{2}{9}, \frac{1}{4}$ (d) $\frac{5}{6}, \frac{7}{9}$ (e) $\frac{5}{12}, \frac{4}{15}$

2 Write each list of fractions in order, smallest first.

(a) $\frac{2}{3}, \frac{7}{10}, \frac{3}{5}$ (b) $\frac{3}{4}, \frac{5}{6}, \frac{7}{9}$ (c) $\frac{2}{9}, \frac{1}{5}, \frac{4}{15}$

3 Work these out.

(a) $\frac{1}{3} + \frac{1}{8}$ (b) $\frac{3}{4} + \frac{1}{5}$ (c) $\frac{1}{3} + \frac{3}{5}$ (d) $\frac{1}{6} + \frac{3}{8}$ (e) $\frac{7}{20} + \frac{1}{3}$

4 Work these out.

(a) $\frac{3}{4} - \frac{5}{12}$ (b) $\frac{3}{8} - \frac{1}{3}$ (c) $\frac{7}{10} - \frac{1}{4}$ (d) $\frac{3}{5} - \frac{1}{7}$ (e) $\frac{5}{6} - \frac{4}{9}$

5 Work these out.

   (a) $1\frac{3}{4} + \frac{1}{3}$ **(b)** $2\frac{1}{3} - \frac{1}{2}$ **(c)** $1\frac{2}{5} + 2\frac{1}{4}$ **(d)** $3\frac{1}{8} - 1\frac{2}{3}$ **(e)** $2\frac{5}{8} + 1\frac{7}{10}$

6 From the fractions in this list find

$\frac{1}{3}$	$\frac{1}{5}$	$\frac{2}{3}$	$\frac{3}{10}$	$\frac{4}{5}$	$\frac{7}{10}$

   (a) the largest   **(b)** the smallest

   (c) a pair whose difference is $\frac{1}{2}$ **(d)** a pair whose sum is $\frac{13}{15}$

D Multiplying a fraction by a whole number
E Dividing a fraction by a whole number

1 Work these out.

   (a) $\frac{1}{2} \times 12$ **(b)** $16 \times \frac{1}{8}$ **(c)** $\frac{1}{5} \times 15$ **(d)** $7 \times \frac{1}{4}$ **(e)** $\frac{1}{3} \times 10$

2 Work these out, giving each result as a mixed number in its simplest form.

   (a) $\frac{3}{4} \times 7$ **(b)** $\frac{4}{5} \times 9$ **(c)** $\frac{3}{5}$ of 11 **(d)** $3 \times \frac{5}{12}$ **(e)** $\frac{2}{9}$ of 15

3 Copy and complete these calculations.

   (a) $\frac{1}{4} \times \blacksquare = 1\frac{1}{4}$ **(b)** $\blacksquare \times 12 = 4$ **(c)** $\blacksquare$ of $20 = 15$ **(d)** $\frac{2}{3}$ of $\blacksquare = 3\frac{1}{3}$

4 Work these out.

   (a) $\frac{1}{3} \div 4$ **(b)** $\frac{1}{2} \div 6$ **(c)** $\frac{3}{4} \div 4$ **(d)** $\frac{3}{5} \div 2$ **(e)** $\frac{5}{6} \div 10$

5 Suneet has $\frac{1}{2}$ of a chocolate bar.
He shares this equally among 3 people.
What fraction of the bar does each person get?

6 Ken walks $\frac{3}{4}$ of a mile each day.
How many miles does he walk in 12 days?

7 Millie cuts $\frac{2}{3}$ of a pizza into 4 equal pieces.
What fraction of the pizza is each piece?

F Fractions of fractions
G Multiplying fractions together

1 Work these out, giving each result in its simplest form.

   (a) $\frac{1}{3}$ of $\frac{1}{8}$ **(b)** $\frac{1}{6}$ of $\frac{1}{5}$ **(c)** $\frac{5}{8}$ of $\frac{1}{3}$ **(d)** $\frac{3}{5}$ of $\frac{2}{3}$ **(e)** $\frac{3}{8}$ of $\frac{4}{9}$

   (f) $\frac{1}{2} \times \frac{1}{7}$ **(g)** $\frac{1}{3} \times \frac{7}{8}$ **(h)** $\frac{3}{4} \times \frac{5}{8}$ **(i)** $\frac{2}{3} \times \frac{3}{8}$ **(j)** $\frac{3}{10} \times \frac{4}{5}$

2 Work these out, giving each result in its simplest form.

   (a) $\frac{1}{3} \times 1\frac{1}{2}$ **(b)** $2\frac{1}{4} \times \frac{1}{3}$ **(c)** $1\frac{1}{2} \times 1\frac{2}{3}$ **(d)** $1\frac{4}{5} \times 2\frac{1}{3}$ **(e)** $2\frac{1}{4} \times 1\frac{1}{5}$

3 Copy and complete these calculations.

(a) $\frac{1}{2} \times \blacksquare = \frac{1}{5}$　　(b) $\frac{3}{4}$ of $\blacksquare = \frac{1}{2}$　　(c) $\frac{2}{3} \times \blacksquare = 1$　　(d) $\blacksquare$ of $2\frac{1}{4} = 1\frac{1}{2}$

H Changing between fractions and decimals　　level 6
I Recurring decimals　　level 6

1 Change each of these decimals to a fraction, in its simplest form.

(a) 0.7　　　(b) 0.72　　　(c) 0.77　　　(d) 0.75　　　(e) 0.725

2 Change each of these fractions to a decimal.

(a) $\frac{13}{50}$　　(b) $\frac{3}{20}$　　(c) $\frac{9}{16}$　　(d) $\frac{5}{6}$　　(e) $\frac{8}{9}$

3 Find three words by rewriting the letters in the order of the numbers, smallest first.

(a)

B	**O**	**K**	**E**	**D**	**A**	**R**	**Y**
0.28	$\frac{7}{20}$	$\frac{1}{5}$	$\frac{1}{4}$	$\frac{1}{2}$	$\frac{2}{5}$	0.45	0.252

(b)

P	**O**	**L**	**Y**	**H**	**E**	**X**	**O**	**N**
0.79	$\frac{17}{20}$	$\frac{3}{4}$	$\frac{7}{10}$	$\frac{4}{5}$	$\frac{19}{20}$	0.6	0.77	$\frac{9}{10}$

(c)

B	**E**	**R**	**O**	**M**	**O**	**N**	**T**
0.2	$\frac{1}{3}$	$\frac{1}{25}$	$\frac{1}{10}$	$\frac{1}{8}$	$\frac{1}{4}$	0.3	0.008

J Mixed questions

1 Work these out.

(a) $\frac{1}{2} + \frac{1}{5}$　　(b) $\frac{1}{2} - \frac{1}{5}$　　(c) $\frac{1}{2} \times \frac{1}{5}$　　(d) $1\frac{1}{2} \times \frac{1}{5}$

2 Work these out.

(a) $\frac{3}{8} + \frac{1}{3}$　　(b) $\frac{3}{8} \times \frac{1}{3}$　　(c) $\frac{3}{8} - \frac{1}{3}$　　(d) $2\frac{3}{8} \times 1\frac{1}{3}$

3 A bottle contains $\frac{3}{4}$ of a litre of wine.
A group of 12 people share three of these bottles equally among themselves.
What fraction of a litre does each person get?

4 Jane has a chocolate bar.
Jane eats $\frac{1}{3}$ of it and a friend eats $\frac{1}{4}$ of the bar.
The remaining chocolate is shared between Jane's two brothers.
What fraction of a bar does each brother get?

5 Parallel lines and angles

A Angles from parallel lines crossing

1 In this diagram, one set of parallel lines
   has been marked with single arrows
   and the other set of parallel lines has been
   marked with double arrows.

   Give the letters for these.

   (a) Two pairs of vertically opposite angles

   (b) Two pairs of corresponding angles

   (c) Two pairs of alternate angles

   (d) Two pairs of supplementary angles

2 Find each angle marked with a **?**, giving a reason.

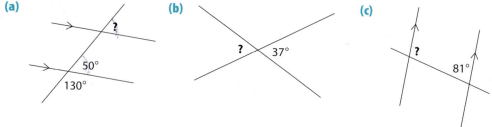

   (a)   **(b)**   **(c)**

3 Work out the value of each angle marked with a letter, giving a reason.

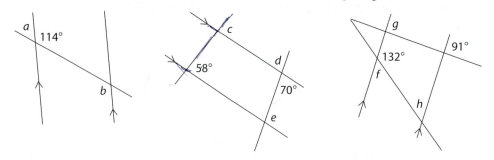

4 **(a)** In a pair of supplementary angles, one angle is 61°.
       What is the other?

   (b) In a pair of alternate angles, one angle is 43°.
       What is the other?

   (c) In a pair of supplementary angles, one angle is four times the size of the other.
       What are their sizes?

1 Work out each angle marked with a small letter, explaining your reasoning.

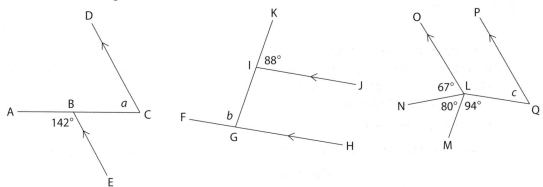

2 Work out each angle marked with a small letter, explaining your reasoning.

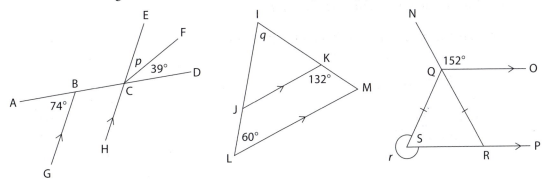

3 Work out each angle marked with a small letter.
You can copy the diagram and draw any extra lines if you need to.
Explain your reasoning.

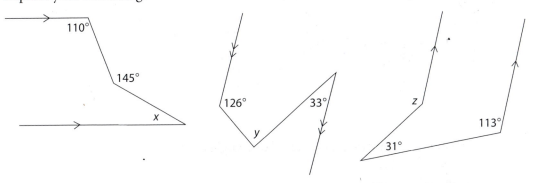

4 P and Q are two ships at sea. The bearing of P from Q is 286°.
Draw a sketch of the situation and use it to find the bearing of Q from P.

6 Percentages

A Percentages, decimals and fractions

1 Write these percentages as fractions, simplifying where possible.

(a) 45%   (b) 6%   (c) 17%   (d) 88%   (e) 80%

2 Find pairs of matching percentages and decimals.

A 0.37   **B** 2.5%   **C** 25%   **D** 30%   **E** 0.03

F 0.25   **G** 37%   **H** 0.3   **I** 0.025   **J** 3%

3 Write these fractions as percentages.

(a) $\frac{13}{50}$ (b) $\frac{84}{200}$ (c) $\frac{9}{25}$ (d) $\frac{8}{40}$ (e) $\frac{21}{30}$

4 Put each set of decimals, percentages and fractions in order, smallest first.

(a) $\frac{3}{4}$ 85% 0.8 $\frac{7}{10}$ 65%   (b) 0.08 $\frac{1}{20}$ 15% 0.2 $\frac{1}{25}$

(c) $\frac{9}{20}$ 0.5 42% $\frac{2}{5}$ $\frac{12}{25}$ (d) 70% 0.6 0.67 $\frac{2}{3}$ 66%

B Percentage of a quantity

1 Work these out.

(a) 24% of 78   (b) 67% of 450   (c) 7% of 35.6

2 In a factory the quality control team tests 8% of the lightbulbs produced.
How many lightbulbs from a batch of 12 500 will be tested?

3 The ingredients for a packet of six chocolate biscuits include 27% wheat flour
and 11% milk chocolate.
A packet of the biscuits weighs 125 g.

(a) What is the weight of wheat flour used in the packet of biscuits?

(b) What is the weight of milk chocolate on each biscuit?

4 Work these out, giving your answers to the nearest penny.

(a) 17.5% of £97   (b) 5.75% of £63.50   (c) 18.6% of £126

5 Geraldine pays a garage a deposit of 37.5% for a car costing £6499.
How much deposit does she pay? (Give your answer to the nearest £1.)

6 Each year Harry has to pay interest of 7.25% on a house loan of £125 000.
How much interest does he pay each year?

c One number as a percentage of another

1 Ashleigh did a survey of the 160 trees in her local park.
She counted 24 oak trees and 40 beech trees, and the rest were chestnut trees.
Calculate the percentage of each type of tree in the park.

2 These are Chloe's scores in three mathematics assessments.
Which was her best result? Show how you decide.

$\dfrac{28}{50}$ $\qquad$ $\dfrac{22}{40}$ $\qquad$ $\dfrac{39}{75}$

3 The table shows the results of a survey
of the reliability of cars.

   (a) For each make of car, calculate
the percentage that broke down.

   (b) Which make was the most reliable?

   (c) How many cars were there in total?

   (d) What percentage of all the cars
broke down?

Number of breakdowns in one year of cars up to six years old		
Make	Sample size	Breakdowns
A	1245	456
B	655	245
C	1456	312
D	890	180
E	386	125

4 In a test, 78 out of a sample of 126 Everlasting batteries ran for over 18 hours
whereas 65 out of a sample of 108 Goodlife batteries ran for more than 18 hours.

   (a) What percentage of each type of battery lasted for over 18 hours?

   (b) What percentage of all the batteries lasted for more than 18 hours?

D Percentage increase and decrease
level 6

1 In a sale all items are reduced by 20%.
What is the sale price of a CD player that originally cost £80?

2 The average August rainfall in a town is 60 mm.
Last August, the rainfall was 25% higher than the average.
What was the rainfall last August?

3 A bag of pasta weighs 500 g.
A special-offer bag is advertised as having 20% extra free.
What is the weight of the special-offer bag of pasta?

E Increasing using a multiplier
F Decreasing using a multiplier

1 What number should you multiply by

   (a) to increase a quantity by 23%

   (b) to decrease a quantity by 15%

   (c) to increase a quantity by 4%

   (d) to decrease a quantity by 2%

2 Increase

    (a) £32 by 15%   **(b)** £840 by 8%   **(c)** £189.40 by 35% **(d)** £230 by 7%

3 Reduce

    (a) £45 by 28%   **(b)** £495 by 7%   **(c)** £842.40 by 85% **(d)** £543 by 13%

4 A worker earns £18 000 per year.
He is to get a 5% pay rise.
What will be his new earnings?

5 The number of people using a travel agency has decreased by 12% over the year.
Last year 3425 visited the travel agency.
How many people visited the travel agency this year?

6 Claire went on a diet and lost 8% of her weight.
Before going on the diet she weighed 75 kg.
What was her weight at the end of the diet?

7 A teenage magazine normally sells 26 000 copies each week.
The editor increased sales by 34% by putting a picture of a pop star on the front cover.
What was the new sales total?

8 The value of a computer has decreased by 35% in the last year.
Last year the computer was worth £1200.
What is the present value of the computer?

9 A sports stadium seats 35 000 people.
The stands are being redeveloped and this will increase the number of seats by 9%.
How many seats will there be in the redeveloped stadium?

10 One year a company gives all employees a pay rise of 4.2%.
Calculate the new salary of an employee whose old salary was £24 500.

G Finding an increase as a percentage
H Finding a decrease as a percentage

1 Daniel's pay increased from £8.50 per hour to £9.35 per hour.
What was the percentage increase in his pay?

2 In 2005 Jennifer drove 6000 miles in her car.
In 2006 she drove 5700 miles.
Find the percentage decrease in miles driven between 2005 and 2006.

3 Between 1982 and 2001, the population of the United Kingdom increased
from 56 million to 60 million.
Calculate the percentage increase.

4 Calculate the percentage change in each case below, correct to the nearest 1%.
Say whether it is an increase or a decrease.

(a) From £35.50 to £37.63

(b) From 7.60 m to 6.46 m

(c) From £6.05 to £4.93

(d) From 560 mm to 615 mm

(e) From £435 to £420

(f) From 338 g to 357 g

5 After doing some fitness exercises, Sarah's pulse rate was 85 beats per minute.
She rested for a while and her pulse rate dropped to 62 beats per minute.
Find the percentage decrease in her pulse rate.

6 In the 1992/93 football season, 9 760 000 people attended Premier league matches.
This increased to 12 880 000 for the 2005/06 season.
Calculate the percentage increase in attendance between 1992/93 and 2005/06.

▎ Mixed questions

1 (a) Ten years ago the sales of a daily newspaper averaged 2 900 000 copies.
Since then sales have dropped by 24%.
What are the current sales, correct to two significant figures?

(b) Over the same period of time, another newspaper has increased its sales
from 1 700 000 copies to 2 400 000 copies.
What is the percentage increase in sales, correct to the nearest 1%?

2 The table records household conveniences in a town in 1996 and 2006.

	1996	2006
Total number of households	15 000	17 800
Households with central heating	12 700	16 800
Households with a washing machine	13 600	16 900
Households with a dishwasher	2 900	6 200

(a) Calculate the percentage of households with central heating in

(i) 1996   (ii) 2006

(b) Calculate the percentage increase between 1996 and 2006 of

(i) the number of households with a washing machine

(ii) the number of households with a dishwasher

(c) In 1996 71% of the households in the town had the use of a car.
Calculate the number of households with the use of a car in 1996.

(d) From 1996 to 2006, the number of households having the use of a car
increased by 23%.
Calculate the number of households in the town having the use of a car in 2006,
correct to three significant figures.

7 Pie charts

You need an angle measurer or a pie chart scale.

A Interpreting pie charts

The constituents of food that give energy are protein, fat and carbohydrate.

The pie charts below show the percentage by weight of these constituents in white bread and in butter.

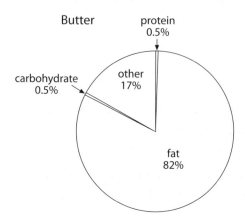

White bread

protein 7.5%
fat 4.5%
other 36.5%
carbohydrate 51.5%

Butter

protein 0.5%
carbohydrate 0.5%
other 17%
fat 82%

1 (a) Complete this statement:
'White bread contains … times as much protein as butter contains.'

(b) A slice of white bread weighs 40 g. How much carbohydrate does it contain?

(c) How much fat is there in 10 g of butter?

*2 Food energy is often given in 'calories'.
Each gram of protein yields 4 calories, each gram of fat 9 calories and each gram of carbohydrate 4 calories.

Calculate how many calories you would get from a 40 g slice of bread spread with 10 g of butter.

B Drawing a pie chart using angles

1 The table shows the number of times each country won the football World Cup between 1930 and 2006.

(a) In a pie chart, how many degrees will represent one win?

(b) Draw a pie chart to show the information.

Argentina	2
Brazil	5
England	1
France	1
Italy	4
Uruguay	2
Germany	3

2 The daily timetable of a Victorian workhouse is shown here.

(a) Copy and complete this table, giving exact angles.

Activity	Number of hours	Angle in pie chart
Work		
Eating		
Prayers		
Bed		
Total	24	360°

6:00 a.m.	Prayers
6:30 a.m.	Breakfast
7:00 a.m.	Work
12:00 noon	Lunch
1:00 p.m.	Work
6:00 p.m.	Supper
7:00 p.m.	Prayers
8:00 p.m.	Bed

(b) Draw a pie chart to show the information.

C Drawing a pie chart using a percentage scale
D Mixed questions

level 6

1 A group of visitors to Thorpe Park were asked to name their favourite ride.

The results are shown in the table.

Draw a pie chart to show this information.
Label each slice with the percentage.

Favourite ride	Number of people
Stealth	36
Colossus	38
Detonator	18
Nemesis Inferno	45
Slammer	26
Total	163

2 This table shows the population of each of the four countries of the UK in 2001.

	England	Wales	Scotland	N. Ireland	Total
Population (millions)	49.4	2.9	5.1	1.6	59.0

Draw a pie chart to show this information.

3 The results of the 2005 British general election are shown in the table.

Party	Number of seats	Percentage of vote
Labour	355	35.2
Conservative	198	32.3
Liberal Democrat	62	22.0
Others	30	10.5
Total	645	100.0

(a) Calculate the percentage of seats won by each party.

(b) Draw two pie charts, one for seats and one for votes.

(c) Comment on the differences between the two charts.

Mixed practice 1

1 Round the number 4 961 527 to the nearest thousand.

2 Work these out.

    (a) 1.2×100 **(b)** $49.3 \div 1000$ **(c)** $0.4 \div 100$

3 Find an approximate answer to 279×3209, showing your working clearly.

4 Jen has 45 packs of buns, each holding 16 buns.
She shares the buns equally among 24 elephants.
How many buns does each elephant get?

5 Work these out, giving each answer in its simplest form where appropriate.

    (a) $\frac{3}{8}$ of 32   **(b)** $\frac{1}{8} + \frac{1}{5}$ **(c)** $\frac{3}{4} - \frac{1}{8}$ **(d)** $16 \times \frac{2}{3}$ **(e)** $\frac{4}{5} \div 3$

    (f) $\frac{5}{6} - \frac{3}{4}$ **(g)** $1\frac{5}{8} \times 2$ **(h)** $\frac{5}{8}$ of 4   **(i)** $\frac{2}{3} \times \frac{9}{16}$ **(j)** $\frac{8}{11} \div 4$

6 Work out each angle marked with a letter, explaining your reasoning.

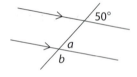 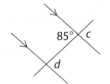 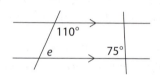

7 Jake and Maia have a bag of sweets.
Jake eats $\frac{1}{4}$ of the sweets and Maia eats $\frac{2}{5}$ of the sweets.

    (a) Who has eaten more sweets, Jake or Maia?

    (b) What percentage of the sweets have they eaten in total?

    (c) What fraction of the sweets is left?

8 Calculate   **(a)** $\frac{0.21}{0.07}$ **(b)** $\frac{2.8}{0.04}$ **(c)** $\frac{0.84}{0.4}$ **(d)** $\frac{0.34}{0.05}$

9 Write these in order, smallest first: 0.3, $\frac{1}{3}$, $\frac{33}{100}$, 3%, 0.027

10 A cat eats $\frac{2}{3}$ of a can of cat food each day.

    (a) How many cans are needed to feed the cat for 12 days?

    (b) How long will 14 cans of cat food last?

11 Work out 8.5% of £18.

12 17 identical marbles weigh 141 g.
How much would 11 of the same marbles weigh?
Give your answer to a sensible degree of accuracy.

13 The value of Mike's car decreased by 17% over the past year.
The car was worth £5600 a year ago.
How much is it worth now?

14 Residents were asked to choose one option to
try to reduce speeding.
The table shows the results of the survey.

(a) Draw a pie chart to show this information.

(b) What percentage of those asked chose
speed cameras?

Proposed solution	Number in favour
Speed humps	164
Narrow points	48
Speed cameras	212
Nothing	65
Total	489

15 Round these numbers to three significant figures.

(a) 25 638   (b) 1 087 342   (c) 3.483 561   (d) 0.004 869 12

16 A cinema reduced its ticket prices and the audience increased by 15%.
Before the price reduction, the weekly attendance at the cinema was 980.
What was the weekly attendance after the reduction in price, correct to the nearest ten?

17 When Jade was born she was 50 centimetres long.
By age 30 she had grown to 1.76 metres tall.
Sketch a graph for Jade's height (h) against time (y) for the first 30 years of her life.

18 The price of a camera increases from £109.50 to £124.50.
What is the percentage increase in price?

19 This is part of a label on some cheese in a supermarket.
What would 500 g of this cheese cost?

Weight	Price
246 g	£1.51

20 Work out the angles marked in blue,
explaining your reasoning

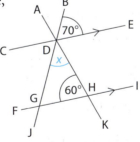

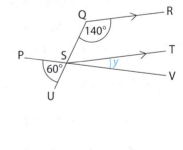

21 In 2006 Jane earned £34 000. In 2007 Jane earned £32 500.
Find the percentage decrease in Jane's earnings between 2006 and 2007.

22 Find the exact value of $\frac{8}{9}$ as a decimal.

23 Tom saw this book on sale at an airport.
He had some pounds and some euros.
He had bought his euros at the rate of 1.55 euros to each pound.

Is it cheaper for him to pay with pounds or with euros?

SPECIAL OFFER!!
€6.99 £4.99
ALICE MAY BELLE

8 Pythagoras's theorem

B Squares on right-angled triangles

1 Work out the missing area in each of these.

(a)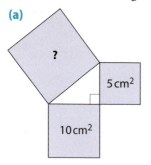

(b)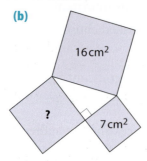

(c)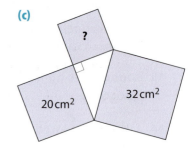

2 Work out the missing area or length in each of these.

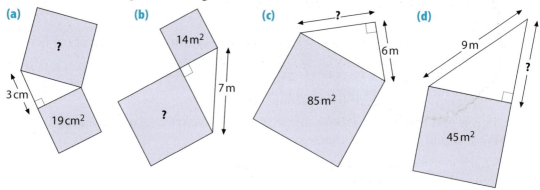

3 Work out the missing lengths.

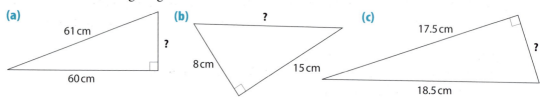

C Square roots – a reminder
D Using Pythagoras

1 Calculate, to the nearest 0.1 cm, the length of the hypotenuse of a right-angled triangle whose other two sides are

    (a) 4 cm and 8 cm   **(b)** 3 cm and 5 cm   **(c)** 6 cm and 7 cm

    (d) 9 cm and 13 cm   **(e)** 7 cm and 7 cm   **(f)** 6 cm and 16 cm

2 Calculate, to the nearest 0.1 cm, the length of the side marked **?** in each of these right-angled triangles.

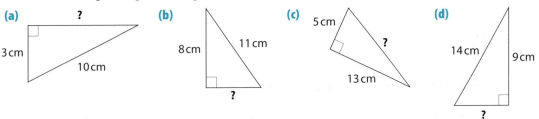

(a) ? 3 cm 10 cm

(b) 8 cm 11 cm ?

(c) 5 cm ? 13 cm

(d) 14 cm 9 cm ?

3 The two shorter sides of a set-square are both 7.4 cm long.
How long is the longest edge? (Give the answer to 1 d.p.)

4 A square has sides 4.5 cm long. How long is each diagonal?

5 The bottom end of a ladder is 3 m from the wall of a house.
The top end reaches 5.5 m up the wall.
Draw a sketch and calculate the length of the ladder.

6 This equilateral triangle has been divided into two
congruent right-angled triangles.

(a) Use Pythagoras's theorem to calculate the height h cm.
Give your answer to three significant figures but
keep the full result on your calculator.

(b) Calculate the area of the equilateral triangle,
to three significant figures.

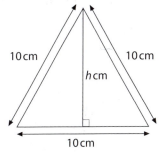

10 cm 10 cm h cm 10 cm

7 Sketch a grid and mark the points P ($^-$2, 1) and Q (5, 3).
Calculate the distance from P to Q, to 2 d.p.

8 Calculate to 2 d.p. the distance between each of these pairs of points.

(a) (0, 2) and (6, 0)   **(b)** (0, 2) and (4, $^-$1)   **(c)** ($^-$2, $^-$4) and (5, $^-$1)

9 A helicopter flies 9 km north from a heliport.
It then flies 14 km west. Finally it flies 12 km south and lands.
How far is it now from the heliport?

10 Calculate the lengths marked with letters.

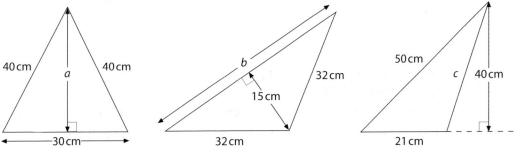

40 cm a 40 cm 30 cm

b 32 cm 15 cm 32 cm

50 cm c 40 cm 21 cm

9 Working with linear expressions

A Substitution

1 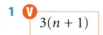   Z $11 - 2n$

V $3(n + 1)$ W $15 - n$ X $\dfrac{n + 3}{2}$ Y $\dfrac{n}{2} + 3$

(a) Find the value of each expression when $n = 3$.

(b) When $n = 0$, which expression has the greatest value?

(c) When $n = 4$, which expression has the greatest value?

(d) When $n = 5$, which expression has the lowest value?

2 Find the value of these expressions when $x = 8$.

(a) $4(2x - 3)$ (b) $\dfrac{2x - 1}{5}$ (c) $15 - \dfrac{3x}{4}$

3 Each expression in the diagram stands for the length of a side in centimetres.

(a) Work out the length of each side when $x = 6$.

(b) What type of triangle is this?

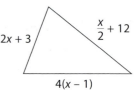

B Simplifying

1 Simplify these expressions.

(a) $6 \times 7n$ (b) $2 \times 8x$ (c) $6 \times 3a$ (d) $8 \times 5b$ (e) $7 \times 9k$

(f) $\dfrac{16y}{8}$ (g) $\dfrac{24c}{3}$ (h) $\dfrac{42h}{7}$ (i) $\dfrac{13m}{13}$ (j) $\dfrac{18p}{9}$

2 Simplify these expressions.

(a) $6 + k + 7 + k$ (b) $5h + 6h - 8h$ (c) $4g + 7 - 2g$ (d) $3d + 6 + d - 1$

(e) $6b + 1 + 2b - 6$ (f) $5a + 4 - 4a - 7$ (g) $3h + 7 - 3h$ (h) $7 + 2x + 9 - 7x$

(i) $9y - 2 - 3y - 5$ (j) $5a + 1 - 6a + 1$ (k) $4 - 2p - 3p + 7$ (l) $7 - 3m - 5 - m$

3 Find and simplify expressions for the perimeters of these shapes.

(a)   (b)   (c)

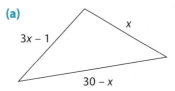   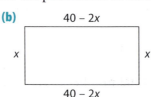   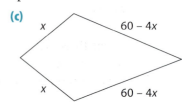

1 Find four pairs of equivalent expressions.

 $2(4a + 12)$ $8a + 8$ **C** $2(3a + 5)$ $8(a + 1)$

E $4(2a + 6)$ **F** $6(a + 1)$ **G** $6a + 10$ **H** $3(2a + 2)$

2 Multiply out the brackets in each of these.

(a) $5(n - 3)$ (b) $3(m + 6)$ (c) $5(2 + x)$ (d) $4(5 - n)$

(e) $3(2b + 4)$ (f) $4(5n - 1)$ (g) $2(6c + 5)$ (h) $3(2 - 5x)$

3 Which of these is an expression for the area of the rectangle?

$3a + 3$ $2a + 12$ $3a + 9$

4 Copy and complete these.

(a) $2(\blacksquare + 4) = 2x + 8$ (b) $3(\blacksquare - 5) = 9p - 15$

(c) $2(\blacksquare + \blacksquare) = 6m + 16$ (d) $\blacksquare(4 + n) = 12 + \blacksquare$

5 Sketch each shape and write an expression for each missing length.

(a) Kite   (b) Rectangle   (c) Equilateral triangle

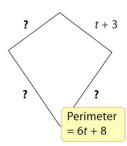   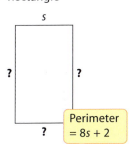   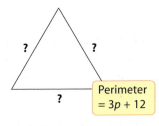

6 Kirk, Josie and Karim have y sweets each.
They are each given 8 more sweets.
Which expression gives the number of sweets they have altogether?

$3y + 8$ $3(y + 8)$ $3(y + 24)$

7 Jamie has three fields with t sheep in each.
10 sheep escape.
Write an expression for the total number of sheep in the fields now.

D Dividing by a number

1 I have six bags of sweets, each with
   n sweets in them.
   I also have 12 loose sweets.
   I share these sweets among three people.

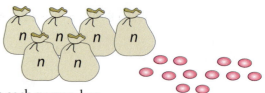

Write an expression for the number of sweets each person has.

2 I have 15 bags of sweets, each with n sweets in them.
   I eat 10 sweets.
   I share the remaining sweets among five people.

Write an expression for the number of sweets each person has.

3 Simplify these expressions.

   (a) $\dfrac{8x - 6}{2}$

   (b) $\dfrac{6a - 12}{3}$

   (c) $\dfrac{14 - 7d}{7}$

   (d) $\dfrac{8b}{2} + 3$

   (e) $9 - \dfrac{6e}{2}$

   (f) $\dfrac{10b}{5} - 3$

4 Simplify these expressions.

   (a) $\frac{1}{2}(4n + 10)$

   (b) $\frac{1}{3}(12n - 9)$

   (c) $\frac{1}{4}(8 - 12n)$

E Justifying number puzzles

1 For each puzzle below …

   (a) Try some numbers and describe what happens.

   (b) Use algebra to explain how the puzzle works.

Puzzle A

Think of a number.
- Add 3.
- Multiply by 2.
- Add 6.
- Divide by 2.
- Subtract 6.

What is the result?

Puzzle B

Think of a number.
- Subtract 2.
- Multiply by 5.
- Add 10.
- Divide by 5.
- Subtract the number
  you first thought of.

What is the result?

Puzzle C

Think of a number.
- Multiply by 3.
- Add 12.
- Divide by 3.
- Subtract the number
  you first thought of.

What is the result?

*2 Make up a puzzle where the final answer is always 8.

10 Representing 3-D objects

You need triangular dotty paper in sections AB and D, and centimetre squared paper in section C.

A The Soma cube   level 6
B Nets   level 6

1 Here are two puzzle pieces made from centimetre cubes.

A 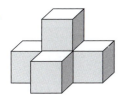   B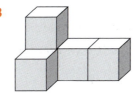

(a) Draw each piece on triangular dotty paper.
     Shade sides that face the same direction in the same way, to help
     show the object more clearly.

(b) What is the volume of each shape?

2 Which of these is a possible net of a cuboid?

A 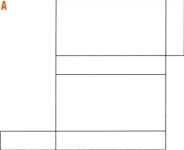   B    C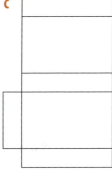

3 These are nets of two 3-D shapes.
   What is the name of each shape?

(a) 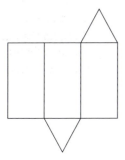   (b)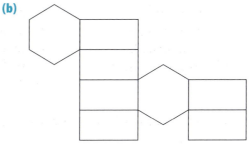

4 A pyramid has a square base with edges of length 5 cm.
Each triangular face is equilateral.
Draw accurately a net of this pyramid.

c Plan and elevations

1 This object has been made from centimetre cubes.
Draw full size on centimetre squared paper

  (a) a plan view

  (b) a side view

  (c) a front view

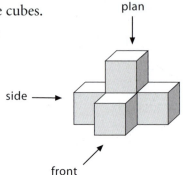

2 This net makes a 3-D object that stands on the face marked 'base'.
Sketch a plan and two elevations of the 3-D object.

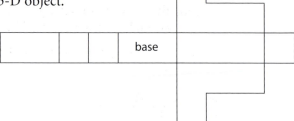

3 This is a sketch of a house.

  (a) On centimetre squared paper, using a scale
    where 1 cm represents 1 m, draw

    (i) a plan view

    (ii) a side view

    (iii) a front view

  (b) By measuring your drawings,
    find the length on the real house
    of the sloping edges AB and CD.

  (c) Calculate, to the nearest 0.01 m,
    the length of AB and CD.

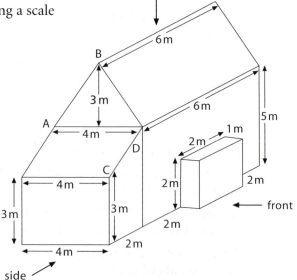

1 Each drawing shows half of a 3-D shape and a plane of symmetry of the whole shape.
Copy each drawing on to triangular dotty paper and complete the shape.

(a)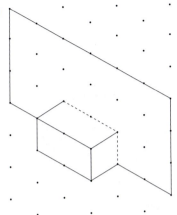

(b)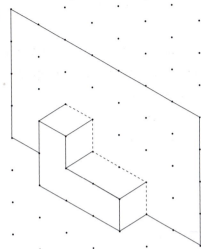

2 For each of the shapes below,

   (i) copy the drawing on triangular dotty paper and show one plane of symmetry
        (it is enough to draw a dotted line on the surface of the shape)

   (ii) state how many planes of symmetry the shape has altogether

(a)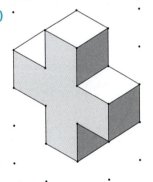

(b)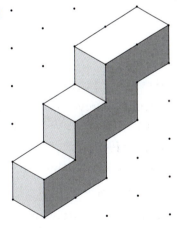

3 This is a sketch of a cuboid with edge lengths a, b and c.

   (a) When a, b and c are all different, how many planes
       of symmetry does the cuboid have?

   (b) When $a = b$ but c is different from a and b, how many
       planes of symmetry does the cuboid have?

   (c) When $a = b = c$, how many planes of symmetry
       does the cuboid have?

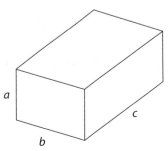

11 Linear equations

A Solving equations

1 Solve each of these equations.

   (a) $4x = 28$ **(b)** $6h + 2 = 20$ **(c)** $2f - 3 = 5$

   (d) $20 - y = 15$ **(e)** $10 - 3n = 7$ **(f)** $30 - 5z = 20$

   (g) $4p - 2 = 4$ **(h)** $8m + 2 = 6$ **(i)** $5 - 2g = 0$

2 Solve each of these equations.

   (a) $3x = x + 8$ **(b)** $6x + 5 = 5x + 6$ **(c)** $4x + 1 = 2x + 11$

   (d) $8x - 3 = 5x + 6$ **(e)** $x + 10 = 7x - 2$ **(f)** $6x - 20 = 3x - 5$

   (g) $4x + 4 = 8x - 2$ **(h)** $9x + 2 = 3x + 23$ **(i)** $3x - 1 = 5x - 2$

3 Solve each of these equations.

   (a) $3n + 5 = 21 - n$ **(b)** $8 - 4n = 3n + 1$ **(c)** $4n - 3 = 27 - 6n$

   (d) $5n - 45 = 11 - 3n$ **(e)** $8 - n = 13 - 2n$ **(f)** $26 - 7n = 10 - 3n$

   (g) $4n + 1 = 10 - 2n$ **(h)** $9 - 3n = 14 - 5n$ **(i)** $2n - 7 = 7 - 2n$

4 Solve each of these equations.

   (a) $5k = 14$ **(b)** $4k - 5 = 10$ **(c)** $9k + 3 = 18 + k$

   (d) $4 + 11k = 9 - 5k$ **(e)** $9 - k = 30 - 13k$ **(f)** $5.9 - 2k = 2.1 + 6k$

B Forming equations from shapes

1 (a) (i) Make a sketch of the triangle for $x = 6$.

     (ii) What is the special name for your triangle?

     (iii) What is its perimeter?

   (b) Find an expression for the perimeter of the triangle.

   (c) What value of x gives a perimeter of 30?

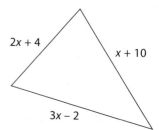

2 The perimeter of this rectangle is 62 cm.
Work out the value of x.

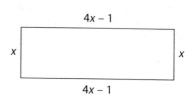

3

(a) Find an expression for the perimeter of this kite.

(b) What value of x gives a perimeter of 36?

4 What value of x gives these triangles the same perimeter?

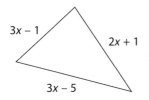 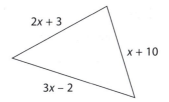

C Solving equations that involve brackets

1 Solve each of these equations.

(a) $2(x + 3) = 14$ (b) $3(x + 5) = 6x$ (c) $3(4x - 3) = 15$

(d) $3(x - 7) = 2x + 1$ (e) $2(x + 3) = 5x - 9$ (f) $3(x + 2) = 2(x + 5)$

(g) $3(2x + 1) = 9(x - 3)$ (h) $2(5x + 1) = 6(2x - 1)$ (i) $4(3x - 1) = 2(4x + 3)$

2 Solve each of these equations.

(a) $2(5 - n) = 4$ (b) $5(20 - 3n) = 10n$ (c) $2(4 - n) = 6(3n - 2)$

(d) $4(n + 3) = 3(11 - n)$ (e) $5(6 - n) = 3(8 - n)$ (f) $3(10 - 3n) = 15(3 - n)$

3 Solve each of these equations.

(a) $5(5k + 1) = 20$ (b) $2(3k - 2) = 7(2k - 3)$ (c) $5(2k - 3) = 5k + 2$

(d) $5(k + 1) = 3(9 - k)$ (e) $3(9 - 2k) = 11(3 - k)$ (f) $5(17 - 3k) = 2(15 - 2k)$

D Solving number puzzles

1 Work out the starting number in each of these 'think of a number' puzzles.

(a)
> I think of a number.
> I subtract 8 and then multiply by 6.
> My answer is double the number I first thought of.

(b)
> I think of a number.
> I add 2 and then multiply by 4.
> My answer is 6 times the number I first thought of.

(c)
> Narinder and Brian both think of the same number.
> Narinder subtracts 5 from her number and multiplies the result by 2.
> Brian multiplies his number by 5 and then subtracts 34.
> They both end up with the same number.

12 Multiples, factors and powers

A Multiples, factors and primes

1 (a) Write down three different factors of 12.

 (b) Write down three different multiples of 12.

2 Give the highest common factor of each of these pairs of numbers.

 (a) 15 and 25 **(b)** 24 and 36 **(c)** 42 and 48 **(d)** 4 and 11

3 Give the lowest common multiple of each of these pairs of numbers.

 (a) 3 and 4 **(b)** 5 and 7 **(c)** 12 and 20 **(d)** 4 and 12

4 List all the prime numbers between 90 and 100.

5 How can you tell that the number 8 940 325 is not prime?

6 Explain why the highest common factor of any pair of different prime numbers is 1.

B Powers

1 Write these using index notation.

 (a) $2 \times 2 \times 2 \times 2$ **(b)** $10 \times 10 \times 10$ **(c)** $7 \times 7 \times 7 \times 7 \times 7$

2 A piece of paper is folded in half so that it is 2 sheets thick.
 It is folded in half again so that it is 4 sheets thick.
 It is folded in half three more times.

 (a) How many sheets thick is it now?

 (b) Write your answer using index notation.

3 Find the value of each of these.

 (a) 3^4 **(b)** 9^2 **(c)** 2^6 **(d)** 10^4 **(e)** 20^3

4 What is the value of 2 to the power of 7?

5 Find the missing numbers in these statements.

 (a) $3^\blacksquare = 27$ **(b)** $7^\blacksquare = 49$ **(c)** $\blacksquare^4 = 625$

6 Choose the correct symbol, $<$, $>$ or $=$, for each box below.

 (a) $4^2 \; \blacksquare \; 2^4$ **(b)** $6^3 \; \blacksquare \; 3^6$ **(c)** $8^2 \; \blacksquare \; 2^8$

7 Calculate these.

    (a) 7^4 **(b)** 5^6 **(c)** 2^{10} **(d)** 15^4 **(e)** 3^9

8 Which is larger, 3^{12} or 12^5?

9 Arrange each set of numbers in order of size, starting with the smallest.

    (a) 6^9 8^8 12^6 14^5 **(b)** 2^{11} 3^7 5^5 7^4

10 Solve these equations.

    (a) $x^5 = 59\,049$ **(b)** $8^x = 4096$ **(c)** $x^8 = 5\,764\,801$

11 What is the largest power of 5 that is less than a million?

12 There is an error in the end digit of each of these calculations. Explain without using a calculator why each calculation cannot possibly be correct.

    (a) $2^{21} = 2\,097\,153$
    (b) $5^8 = 390\,623$
    (c) $4^8 = 65\,530$
    (d) $6^{10} = 60\,466\,174$

c Multiplying powers

1 Find three pairs of equivalent expressions.

  A 35×3^3 **B** 3^{10} **C** $3^9 \times 3$ **D** 3^8 **E** $3^{10} \times 3^5$ **F** 3^{15}

2 Write the answers to these using indices.

    (a) $3^5 \times 3^8$ **(b)** $2^7 \times 2^3 \times 2^5$ **(c)** $4^3 \times 4^5 \times 4$ **(d)** $9 \times 9^4 \times 9$

3 Find the missing numbers in these statements.

    (a) $5^3 \times 5^{\blacksquare} = 5^9$ **(b)** $7^5 \times 7^{\blacksquare} = 7^7$ **(c)** $4 \times 4^{\blacksquare} = 4^4$

4 Find the two **true** statements.

  A $2^2 \times 3^5 \times 2^4 \times 3 = 2^6 \times 3^6$ **B** $3^9 \times 5^3 \times 3^5 = 15^{17}$

  C $4^3 \times 2^4 = 8^7$ **D** $4^3 \times 3^4 \times 4 \times 4^2 \times 3^3 = 4^6 \times 3^7$

5 Copy and complete these statements.

    (a) $3 \times 7^2 \times 3^3 \times 3^4 \times 7 = 3^{\blacksquare} \times 7^{\blacksquare}$ **(b)** $4^2 \times 5 \times 4^5 \times 5^4 = 4^{\blacksquare} \times 5^{\blacksquare}$
    (c) $5^{\blacksquare} \times 4 \times 4^{\blacksquare} \times 5^3 = 4^5 \times 5^5$ **(d)** $3^{\blacksquare} \times 9^{\blacksquare} \times 9^2 \times 3 = 3^4 \times 9^5$

6 Simplify these.

    (a) $10^2 \times 9^4 \times 10 \times 9^5$ **(b)** $5^3 \times 6^3 \times 5^4$ **(c)** $4^3 \times 7 \times 4^4 \times 7^5$

1 Find the prime factorisation of each of these numbers and write it using index notation.

(a) 36   (b) 450   (c) 441   (d) 1008   (e) 600

2 The prime factorisation of 560 is $2 \times 2 \times 2 \times 2 \times 5 \times 7$.
Without doing any calculation, decide which of these are factors of 560.
Show how you decided.

     2, 8, 6, 10, 16, 9, 20, 35, 70, 60, 15, 14, 140

3 The prime factorisation of 1050 is $2 \times 3 \times 5 \times 5 \times 7$.

The prime factorisation of 13 650 is $2 \times 3 \times 5 \times 5 \times 7 \times 13$.

Without doing any calculation, decide whether 13 650 is a multiple of 1050.
Show how you decided.

4 49 000 can be written as $2^r \times 5^s \times 7^t$.
Find r, s and t.

5 The prime factorisation of 924 is $2^2 \times 3 \times 7 \times 11$.
Without doing any calculation, decide which of these are factors of 924.

| 2 | $2^3 \times 3$ | $3^2 \times 7$ | $2^2 \times 7$ | 3×11 | $7^2 \times 11$ | 2×11 |

6 Given that $207 = 3^2 \times 23$, find all six factors of 207.

7 (a) (i) Find the prime factorisation of 12.   **(ii)** Find the prime factorisation of 15.

     (b) Use your prime factorisations to find

         (i) the LCM of 12 and 15   **(ii)** the HCF of 12 and 15

8 Use prime factorisation to find the LCM of each of these.

(a) 20 and 32   (b) 18 and 24   (c) 45 and 120   (d) 36 and 108

9 Use prime factorisation to find the HCF of each of these.

(a) 24 and 54   (b) 80 and 620   (c) 372 and 198   (d) 420 and 560

10 A packet of sweets can be shared equally among 2 or 3 or 4 or 5 people.
What is the smallest number of sweets that could be in the packet?

*11 The HCF of a pair of two-digit numbers is 4.
The LCM of the same pair of numbers is 308.
Find the pair of numbers.

*12 A cuboid 144 mm long, 126 mm wide and 108 mm high is cut up into identical cubes.
What is the smallest possible number of cubes?

13 Negative numbers

A Calculating with positive and negative numbers
level 6

1 Work these out.

(a) ⁻3 – 4   (b) ⁻3 + ⁻2   (c) 5 – 7   (d) 6 – ⁻4   (e) ⁻7 – ⁻2

(f) 3 × ⁻4   (g) ⁻2 × ⁻3   (h) ⁻12 ÷ 4   (i) 27 ÷ ⁻3   (j) 4 × ⁻2 × ⁻1

2 (a) Choose three numbers from this set
to make the highest product.

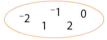

$$\boxed{} \times \boxed{} \times \boxed{}$$

(b) Choose three numbers from the set to make the lowest product.

3 Find the next two numbers in each sequence.

(a) 13, 10, 7, 4, …   (b) ⁻21, ⁻16, ⁻11, ⁻6, …   (c) 7, 5.5, 4, 2.5, 1, …

4 (a) The addition below can be completed using
three different numbers from the loop.

$$\boxed{} + \boxed{} = \boxed{}$$

There are four different additions you can make like this.
List them all.

> Note that, for example,
> ⁻2 + 1 is the same as 1 + ⁻2

(b) The subtraction here can be completed using
three different numbers from the loop.

$$\boxed{} - \boxed{} = \boxed{}$$

There are eight different subtractions you can make like this.
List them all.

5 Work these out.

(a) $4 \times (⁻3 - ⁻7)$ (b) $(⁻2)^3$ (c) $⁻6 + 2 \times ⁻4$ (d) $(⁻5)^2 - 8$

(e) $\dfrac{⁻5 + 3}{2}$ (f) $\dfrac{⁻12 - 6}{⁻3}$ (g) $⁻4 - \dfrac{⁻20}{5}$ (h) $\dfrac{⁻16}{⁻2} + ⁻7$

6 In this puzzle find the four numbers from
this set that fit the clues below.

3	4	1	6	2
⁻3	⁻4	⁻1	⁻6	⁻2

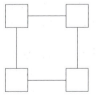

Clue 1:   The product of the numbers in the top row is ⁻12.
Clue 2:   The sum of the numbers in the left-hand column is ⁻3.
Clue 3:   The numbers in the right-hand column are multiples of 2.
Clue 4:   The sum of the numbers in the bottom row is 1.

B Substitution

1 What is the value of each expression when $t = 3$?

(a) $3t - 10$ (b) $12 - 5t$ (c) $8 - t^2$ (d) $5t - 20$ (e) $4(^-2 - t)$

2 Find the value of each expression when $s = {}^-2$.

(a) $3s + 1$ (b) $s^2 + 3$ (c) $5 - s$ (d) $2(s + 3)$ (e) s^3

3 Find the value of each expression when $m = {}^-4$.

(a) $\dfrac{m}{2} + 1$ (b) $(m - 2)^2$ (c) $\dfrac{m^2}{4} - 8$ (d) $2m^2 - 10$ (e) $\dfrac{8 - 3m}{5}$

4 Copy and complete this table for $h = 5 - p^2$.

p	$^-3$	$^-2$	$^-1$	0	1	2	3	4
$h = 5 - p^2$	$^-4$							

5

$2(p + 1)$	$\dfrac{1 - p}{2}$	$2p^2 - 10$	$\dfrac{p^3}{4}$	$\dfrac{p^2 - 5}{^-4}$	$8 - p^2$

(a) When $p = {}^-2$, three expressions above have a value of $^-2$.
Find these expressions.

(b) When $p = 3$, three expressions above have the same value.
Find these expressions.

C Equations with negative solutions

1 (a) Solve the equation $3k + 8 = 2$.

(b) Check that your answer fits the original equation.

2 Solve each of these equations. Check each of your answers.

(a) $5b + 12 = 7$ (b) $3t + 2 = {}^-10$ (c) $5y + 6 = {}^-9$

(d) $3p + 7 = 2p + 5$ (e) $2t + 1 = 5t + 10$ (f) $3z + 4 = 2z - 1$

3 Solve and check each of these.

(a) $9 + h = 5 - h$ (b) $3 - r = 11 + r$ (c) $13 + 2d = 7 - d$

(d) $3j + 13 = 3 - 2j$ (e) $7 - t = 4 - 2t$ (f) $13 - 2z = 1 - 5z$

4 Solve and check each of these.

(a) $2(p + 3) = 4$ (b) $3(q + 4) = q + 6$ (c) $5(r + 4) = 3r$

(d) $3(2s - 1) = 7s + 4$ (e) $5(t + 2) = 3t + 7$ (f) $2(1 - v) = 3(v + 4)$

14 Drawing and using linear graphs

You need graph paper for both sections.

A Drawing straight-line graphs

1 Some of these equations will give you a graph that is a straight line.
From the set below, write down all the equations that give straight-line graphs.

 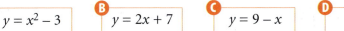

| **A** $y = x^2 - 3$ | **B** $y = 2x + 7$ | **C** $y = 9 - x$ | **D** $x = {}^-3$ | **E** $y = 5$ |

| **F** $y = 3x + 5$ | **G** $y = 10 + x$ | **H** $y = 3x^2$ | **I** $x + y = 8$ |

2 **(a)** Copy and complete this table for $y = 2x + 1$.

x	$^-2$	0	2
$2x + 1$			

(b) On graph paper, draw axes with x from $^-3$ to 3 and y from $^-6$ to 8.
Draw and label the graph of $y = 2x + 1$.

(c) Copy and complete this table for $y = 3 - x$.

x	$^-2$	0	2
$3 - x$			

(d) On your diagram for part (b), draw and label the graph of $y = 3 - x$.

(e) What are the coordinates of the point where the two graphs meet, correct to 1 d.p.?

3 **(a)** Is the point $(2, 5)$ on the graph of $y = 2$?

(b) Is the point $(3, 2)$ on the graph of $y = 2$?

4 On a suitable set of axes, draw and label the graphs of these equations.

(a) $x = 1$ **(b)** $y = 1$ **(c)** $x = {}^-3$ **(d)** $y = {}^-3$

5 A straight line has the equation $2x + 3y = 12$.

(a) Find the value of y when $x = 0$.

(b) Find the value of x when $y = 0$.

(c) Draw the graph using axes with both x and y labelled from 0 to 6.

(d) Use your graph to find the value of x when $y = 3$.

6 **(a)** Copy and complete this table for $5x + 2y = 10$.

x	$^-2$	0	2
y			

(b) Draw axes with x from $^-2$ to 4 and suitable values of y.
On your axes draw the graph of $5x + 2y = 10$.

(c) From your graph, what is the value of y when $x = 1$?

7 Draw axes with both x and y labelled from $^-10$ to 10.
Draw the graph of each of these.

(a) $y = 3x - 5$ (b) $y = 9 - x$ (c) $x = ^-8$

(d) $y = \frac{1}{5}x - 1$ (e) $y = 7$ (f) $2x + y = 8$

8 (a) On a suitable set of axes, draw the graphs of $x + y = 5$ and $y = 3 - \frac{1}{2}x$.

(b) Give the coordinates of the point where the graphs cross.

B Using graphs to solve problems
level 6

1 Lend-a-Hand is a company offering to help with any job.
The formula they use for working out the charge for a job is

$c = 6t + 5$

where c is the charge in £ and t is the time in hours.

(a) What is the charge for 2 hours of help?

(b) Copy and complete this table for Lend-a-Hand.

Time in hours (t)	1	2	3	4	5	6	7	8
Charge in £ (c)								

(c) Draw axes with t going across from 0 to 8 and c going up from 0 to 60.
Plot the points from your table and join them.
Label the graph Lend-a-Hand.

(d) Use your graph to find the charge for a time of $3\frac{1}{2}$ hours.

(e) Use your graph to find how much time you could buy for £50.

2 We're Cheaper is a rival company.
The formula they use for working out the charge for a job is

$c = 7t + 1$

where c is the charge in £ and t is the time in hours.

(a) What is the cost of 2 hours of help with We're Cheaper?

(b) Copy and complete this table for We're Cheaper.

Time in hours (t)	1	2	3	4	5	6	7	8
Charge in £ (c)								

(c) On the same axes that you used for question 1, draw a graph for We're Cheaper.

(d) Estimate how much time you could buy for £25 with We're Cheaper.

(e) Use the graphs to say which company would be cheaper for $2\frac{1}{2}$ hours.
Explain your answer.

(f) How do the graphs show that both companies will charge the same for 4 hours?

15 Using a calculator

| A **Brackets and order of operations** | level 5 |
| B **Division** | level 5 |

A Brackets and order of operations   level 5
B Division   level 5

1 Do these on a calculator.
Round each answer to two decimal places.

   (a) $6.84 + 0.72 \times 1.95$ **(b)** $(3.84 - 1.92) \times 1.67$ **(c)** $20.84 - 15.72 \times 0.85$

   (d) $7.32 \times (9.41 - 2.65)$ **(e)** $8.6 + 9.71 \times 3.8 - 7.4$ **(f)** $0.87 \times 9.21 - 0.24 \times 3.68$

2 Do these on a calculator.
Round each answer to three significant figures.

   (a) $\dfrac{14.7 - 9.6}{2.8}$ **(b)** $3.47 + \dfrac{11.62}{0.59}$ **(c)** $\dfrac{12.31 - 4.76}{5.84 + 1.37}$

   (d) $\dfrac{18.70}{9.42 - 1.48}$ **(e)** $\dfrac{20.5 + 1.4}{15.7 - 10.9}$ **(f)** $\dfrac{16.5}{0.83} - \dfrac{14.8}{0.92}$

C Checking by rough estimates   level 6
D Other keys

1 (a) Arjun wants to get a rough estimate for $\dfrac{48.7 \times 0.38}{0.52}$.

   (i) Write down a calculation Arjun could do to get a rough estimate.

   (ii) Work out the rough estimate without using a calculator.

  (b) Use a calculator to work out $\dfrac{48.7 \times 0.38}{0.52}$, giving the answer to three significant figures.

2 For each calculation below

   (i) work out a rough estimate   **(ii)** calculate the result, to three significant figures

   (a) $\dfrac{88.7 \times 0.58}{11.2}$ **(b)** $\dfrac{624 \times 0.284}{31.7 - 9.8}$ **(c)** $\dfrac{621}{41.5 \times 28.8}$

3 Use a calculator for each of these.
Give each answer correct to two decimal places.

   (a) $(^-6.04)^2$ **(b)** $4.83^2 + 9.71^2$ **(c)** $3 \times \sqrt{8}$ **(d)** $\sqrt{\dfrac{8}{3}}$

4 Use a calculator for each of these.
Give each answer correct to three significant figures.

   (a) $\dfrac{12.7}{(6.2 - 1.8)^2}$ **(b)** $\dfrac{\sqrt{58.2 - 11.7}}{5.3}$ **(c)** $\sqrt{\dfrac{13.6}{12.9 - 5.8}}$ **(d)** $\dfrac{1.56^2}{\sqrt{2.83} + 0.64}$

16 Changing the subject

A Forming and using formulas   level 5

1 Mark is doing some tiling with black and grey tiles.
He arranges the tiles in rows like this.

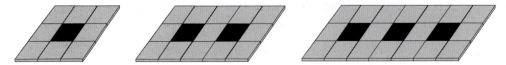

    (a) Copy and complete this table for his rows of tiles.

Number of black tiles (b)	1	2	3	4	5
Number of grey tiles (g)			18		

    (b) Explain why the formula connecting b and g is $g = 5b + 3$.

    (c) Use the formula to find the number of grey tiles needed for a row with

        (i) 10 black tiles   **(ii)** 25 black tiles   **(iii)** 100 black tiles

    (d) Mark uses 103 grey tiles in one of these designs.
        Put $g = 103$ into the formula $g = 5b + 3$.
        Solve the equation you get to find b.

2 Mark uses another design.

    (a) Copy and complete the table for the black and grey tiles in this design.

Number of black tiles (b)	1	2	3	4	5
Number of grey tiles (g)			8		

    (b) Write a formula connecting b and g.

    (c) Use your formula to say how many grey tiles are needed for

        (i) 12 black tiles   **(ii)** 35 black tiles

    (d) Mark uses 150 grey tiles in one of these designs.
        Put $g = 150$ into your formula.
        Solve the equation you get to find the number of black tiles he uses.

    (e) How many black tiles would there be in a design that uses 1000 grey tiles?

1 Mark uses another tile design.

The formula for this pattern is $g = 3b + 3$.
g stands for the number of grey tiles and b stands for the number of black tiles.

(a) What is the value of g when $b = 30$?

(b) Rearrange the formula to make b the subject.

(c) What is the value of b when $g = 33$?

(d) How many black tiles are needed for 78 grey tiles?

2 Another arrangement of black and grey tiles has the formula $g = 4b + 1$.

(a) Rearrange the formula $g = 4b + 1$ to make b the subject.

(b) Work out b when $g = 61$.

(c) How many black tiles will be needed for 85 grey tiles?

3 (a) In the formula $g = 6b + 5$, find g when $b = 10$.

(b) Rearrange the formula $g = 6b + 5$ to make b the subject.

(c) Check the rearrangement is correct by substituting
the value of g from part (a) into your new formula.

(d) Work out b when $g = 101$.

4 Make the bold letter the subject of each of these formulas.

(a) $y = 3\boldsymbol{x} + 7$ (b) $f = 4\boldsymbol{g} + 11$ (c) $j = 5\boldsymbol{k}$ (d) $p = 15 + 7\boldsymbol{q}$

(e) $y = 6\boldsymbol{x} + 5$ (f) $c = \boldsymbol{d} + 9$ (g) $h = 25 + 9\boldsymbol{m}$ (h) $5\boldsymbol{v} + 3 = u$

5 Which of the following is a correct rearrangement of $y = 3b - 5$?

A $b = \dfrac{y - 5}{3}$ B $b = \dfrac{5 - y}{3}$ C $b = \dfrac{y + 3}{5}$ D $b = \dfrac{y + 5}{3}$ E $b = \dfrac{y - 3}{5}$

6 Make the bold letter the subject of each of these formulas.

(a) $y = 2\boldsymbol{x} - 1$ (b) $f = 7\boldsymbol{g} - 10$ (c) $j = \boldsymbol{k} - 5$ (d) $p = 5\boldsymbol{q} - 6$

(e) $y = 9\boldsymbol{x} - 4$ (f) $c = \boldsymbol{d} - 8$ (g) $h = 4\boldsymbol{m} - 3$ (h) $9\boldsymbol{v} - 2 = u$

7 Rearrange each of these formulas to make the bold letter the subject.

(a) $y = 5\boldsymbol{x} + 9$ (b) $f = 4\boldsymbol{g} - 10$ (c) $p = 12 + 3\boldsymbol{q}$ (d) $t = 3\boldsymbol{s} - 7$

(e) $y = 4\boldsymbol{x}$ (f) $u = 7\boldsymbol{v} - 12$ (g) $8\boldsymbol{u} + 2 = v$ (h) $10\boldsymbol{g} - 3 = h$

17 Grid totals

A Expressions from patterns on a number grid

1 This grid of numbers has ten columns.
Sam's C-shape outlines some numbers.

She calculates the 'C-total' by
adding the numbers in the shape.

1	2	3	4	5	6	7	8	9	10
11	12	13	14	15	16	17	18	19	20
21	22	23	24	25	26	27	28	29	30
31	32	33	34	35	36	37	38	39	40
41	42	43	44	45	46	47	48	49	50

15	16
25	
35	36

The C-total is $15 + 16 + 25 + 35 + 36 = 127$.

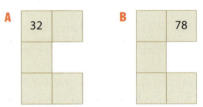

(a) Suppose the grid is continued downwards.

   (i) Copy and complete these C-shapes.

   (ii) Find the C-total for each one.

(b) Sam labels the number in the top left of the C as n.

   (i) Copy and complete this C-shape for the grid above.

   (ii) Write an expression for the C-total on this grid.

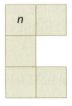

   (iii) What numbers are in the C-shape when the C-total is 552?

   (iv) Explain why you cannot have a C-shape with a total of 100 on this grid.

2 Another grid of numbers has **eight** columns.

1	2	3	4	5	6	7	8
9	10	11	12	13	14	15	16
17	18	19	20	21	22	23	24
25	26	27	28	29	30	31	32

(a) Copy and complete this C-shape for the eight-column grid.

(b) Write an expression for the C-total.

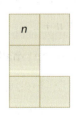

(c) Show that no C-total on this grid can be a multiple of 5.

Mixed practice 2

You need centimetre squared paper and graph paper.

1 Calculate these.

(a) $^-3 + {}^-4$ (b) $5 + {}^-7$ (c) $6 - {}^-5$ (d) $^-2 - {}^-6$

(e) $^-6 \times 4$ (f) $^-5 \times {}^-4$ (g) $^-20 \div 4$ (h) $^-20 \div {}^-4$

(i) $(6-9) \times 5$ (j) $\dfrac{^-12}{6} + 1$ (k) $5 - \dfrac{^-9}{3}$ (l) $\dfrac{6 + {}^-10}{^-2}$

2 Write $5 \times 5 \times 5 \times 5 \times 5 \times 5 \times 5$ in shorthand form using an index.

3 What is the equation of the straight line joining the points $(3, 6)$ and $(3, {}^-6)$?

4 What is the value of each expression when $n = 12$?

(a) $2n + 5$ (b) $20 - n$ (c) $\dfrac{3n - 8}{2}$ (d) $\dfrac{2n}{3}$ (e) $5 - \dfrac{n}{4}$

5 Work out the missing length in this right-angled triangle.

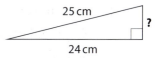

6 This object has been made from eight centimetre cubes. Draw full size on centimetre squared paper

(a) a plan view

(b) a side view

(c) a front view

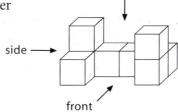

7 Simplify these expressions.

(a) $3x \times 6$ (b) $6 + 8p - 3 - 10p$ (c) $\dfrac{20n}{5} + 1$ (d) $\dfrac{8t + 14}{2}$

8 (a) Write down all the factors of 35.

(b) Find the highest common factor of 35 and 49.

(c) (i) Find the lowest common multiple of 35 and 49.

(ii) Calculate $\frac{1}{35} + \frac{1}{49}$.

9 Multiply out the brackets in these.

(a) $3(n + 2)$ (b) $5(6 - x)$ (c) $2(3m - 1)$ (d) $9(2y + 3)$

10 What is the smallest power of 7 that is greater than a million?

11 Make the bold letter the subject of each formula.

(a) $A = 2\boldsymbol{r} + 5$ (b) $h = 7 + 4\boldsymbol{k}$ (c) $a = \boldsymbol{b} - 10$ (d) $y = 6\boldsymbol{x} - 1$

12 Calculate the area of the shaded square in this diagram.

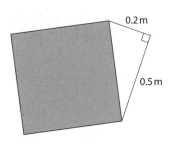

0.2 m

0.5 m

13 Copy and complete these statements.

(a) $3^{\blacksquare} = 81$

(b) $\blacksquare^9 = 1$

(c) $7^{\blacksquare} \times 7^3 = 7^5$

(d) $2^3 \times 5^{\blacksquare} = 200$

(e) $11 \times 11^2 \times 11^3 = 11^{\blacksquare}$

(f) $2^{\blacksquare} \times 3^{\blacksquare} \times 2^7 \times 3 = 2^{10} \times 3^{10}$

14 Find the value of each expression when $n = {}^-2$.

(a) $2n + 9$

(b) $3(n - 1)$

(c) $5(2n + 1)$

(d) $6(1 - n)$

(e) $\dfrac{n + 7}{2}$

(f) $\dfrac{n^2}{4} - 3$

(g) $(n - 4)^2$

(h) $\dfrac{10 - 4n}{9}$

15 Work out the missing lengths, giving your answers to one decimal place.

(a)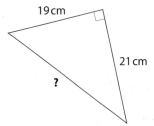

19 cm

21 cm

?

(b)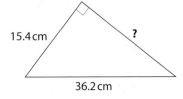

15.4 cm

?

36.2 cm

16 Use graph paper for this question.

(a) On a suitable set of axes, draw the graphs of $x + 2y = 12$ and $y = 2x - 5$.

(b) Estimate the coordinates of the point where the graphs cross.

17 (a) Find and simplify an expression for the perimeter of this rectangle.

x

$2x + 13$

(b) Find the length of the rectangle when the perimeter is 41.

18 A rectangle measures 10 cm by 3 cm.
Calculate the length of one of its diagonals, to the nearest 0.1 cm.

19 The cost, C pence, of printing n party invitations is given by $C = 150 + 50n$.

(a) What is the cost of printing 20 invitations?

(b) Rearrange this formula to make n the subject.

(c) How many invitations could you get printed for £20?

20 Solve the equation $x^5 = 59\,049$.

21 Calculate each of these, giving the result to two decimal places.

(a) $\dfrac{7.69 - 2.92}{2.8}$

(b) $\dfrac{3.04}{4.2 \times 0.85}$

(c) $\dfrac{2.81 - \sqrt{11.4}}{9}$

(d) $\sqrt{19.6 \times 4.2^2}$

(e) $(6.7 - 9.8)^2$

(f) $\sqrt{3.3^2 + 0.8^2 - 1.8^2}$

22 Solve these equations.

(a) $7x + 2 = 4x + 11$

(b) $8x - 3 = 3x + 7$

(c) $5(2 + x) = 7x + 9$

(d) $5n + 1 = 9n - 17$

(e) $13 - 3n = 5n + 1$

(f) $2(n - 1) = 5 - 3n$

(g) $3(y + 5) = 10(y - 2)$

(h) $3(5 + y) = 2y + 13$

(i) $y + 12 = 6 - 2y$

23 The diagram shows the net of a right-angled triangular prism.

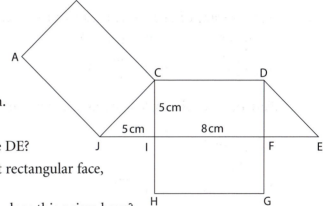

The net is folded to make the prism.

(a) Which points are joined to G?

(b) Which side is joined to the side DE?

(c) Calculate the area of the largest rectangular face, correct to $0.1\,\text{cm}^2$.

(d) How many planes of symmetry does this prism have?

24 (a) Write 198 as a product of prime factors using index notation.

(b) Use the product to decide whether 13 is a factor of 198. Explain how you decided.

(c) (i) What is the highest common factor of 30 and 198?

(ii) What is the lowest common multiple of 7 and 198?

25 Calculate the length of the straight line joining the points $(^-3, \,^-2)$ and $(1, 9)$.

26 (a) (i) Think of a number.
Multiply by 2, add 10 and then multiply by 3.
Now divide by 6 and take away the number you first thought of.
What is your result?

(ii) Repeat part (i) with some different starting numbers.

(iii) Describe what happens each time.

(b) Use algebra to explain the results of part (a).

***27** What is the last digit of   (a) 11^{50} (b) 12^{100}

18 Ratio

A Writing a ratio in its simplest form
level 5

1 A recipe for cranberry sauce uses 175 g of cranberries and 75 g of sugar.

    (a) Write the ratio of cranberries to sugar in its simplest form.

    (b) Write the ratio of sugar to cranberries in its simplest form.

2 Write each of these ratios in its simplest form.

    (a) 3:12   **(b)** 6:30   **(c)** 24:8   **(d)** 12:16   **(e)** 14:12

    (f) 48:56   **(g)** 12:27   **(h)** 100:35   **(i)** 32:20   **(j)** 40:24

3 Mark mixes 250 ml of orange squash with 1 litre of water.
Write the ratio of squash to water in its simplest form.

4 Simplify these ratios as far as possible.

    (a) 60 cm:1 m   **(b)** 5 mm:2 cm   **(c)** 500 g:1 kg   **(d)** 4 m:80 cm

    (e) 400 m:2 km   **(f)** 5 m:25 cm   **(g)** 400 ml:3 litres   **(h)** 5 cm:4 mm

5 Match up these ratios in pairs.

| 1:3:6 | 25:75:100 | 10:20:40 | 5:15:20 | 5:15:30 | 3:6:12 |

6 A recipe for muesli uses 225 g oats, 100 g raisins and 75 g hazelnuts.
Write the ratio oats:raisins:hazelnuts in its simplest form.

7 Sunita is making samosas.
For the filling she mixes 1.5 kg potatoes with 750 g peas and 500 g onions.
Write the ratio potatoes:peas:onions in its simplest form.

B Finding a value from a given ratio
level 6
C Dividing in a given ratio
level 6

1 Soft blue paint is made by mixing blue and white in the ratio 1:4.
Copy and complete this mixing table.

Blue (1 part)	White (4 parts)
2 litres	
	12 litres
0.5 litre	
	10 litres

2 At a party, the ratio of children to adults is 6:1.
If there are 30 children, how many adults are there?

3 Spring green paint is made by mixing yellow and blue in the ratio 4:3.
Copy and complete this mixing table.

Yellow (4 parts)	Blue (3 parts)
8 litres	
	9 litres
2 litres	
	7.5 litres

4 Tracy and May share £150 in the ratio 2:3.
How much does each of them get?

5 To make shortcrust pastry, Nigel mixes 1 part fat with 2 parts flour.
He wants to make 750 g of pastry.

(a) How much fat will he need?   **(b)** How much flour will he need?

6 Asif wants to use 3 red blocks for every 5 grey blocks in his patio.
If he uses 300 grey blocks, how many red blocks will he use?

7 Copy this table and complete the quantities.

Ratio	Quantities
1:2	…m : 400 m
2:5	10 kg : … kg
4:7	16 cm : … cm
10:9	… g : 45 g

8 (a) Divide £24 in the ratio 1:5.   **(b)** Divide 32 m in the ratio 5:3.

(c) Share 45 kg in the ratio 2:7.   **(d)** Share £12 in the ratio 3:2.

9 When planting garden tubs, Laura uses 3 marigolds for every 2 lobelia plants.

(a) If Laura has 30 marigolds, how many lobelia does she need?

(b) If she has 18 lobelia, how many marigolds does she need?

10 A book is to be produced with colour and black-and-white pages in the ratio 1:3.
The book is 144 pages long.

(a) How many colour pages are there?

(b) How many black-and-white pages are there?

11 Laura mixes loam, peat and sand in the ratio 7:3:2 for her potting compost.
If she has 35 litres of loam, how much peat and how much sand does she need?

12 A box of wooden bricks contains red, blue and yellow bricks in the ratio 5:3:2.
There are 300 bricks in the box.
How many of each colour are there?

13 (a) Divide £48 in the ratio 3:4:1.   **(b)** Divide £120 in the ratio 2:3:1.

14 The numbers of children, adults and senior citizens in a cinema are in the ratio 3:5:1.
There are 216 people in the cinema altogether.
How many adults are there in the cinema?

D Converting between ratios, fractions and percentages level 6

1 A bag of peppers contains red peppers and green peppers in the ratio $1:2$.
What fraction of the peppers are **(a)** red **(b)** green

2 In a pick-a-straw game, $\frac{1}{5}$ of the straws win prizes.
What is the ratio of winning to losing straws?

3 The ratio of boys to girls in a drama club is $1:3$.

(a) What fraction of the club are boys? **(b)** What percentage are girls?

4 $\frac{2}{3}$ of the puppies in a dogs' home are male.
What is the ratio of male to female puppies?

5 The ratio of fiction to non-fiction books in a library is $3:2$.
What percentage of the books are non-fiction?

6 Boxes contain dark and milk chocolates.
Put these statements into pairs so that the statements in each pair say the same thing.

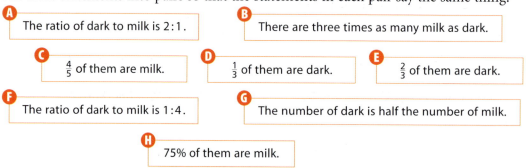

A The ratio of dark to milk is $2:1$.

B There are three times as many milk as dark.

C $\frac{4}{5}$ of them are milk.

D $\frac{1}{3}$ of them are dark.

E $\frac{2}{3}$ of them are dark.

F The ratio of dark to milk is $1:4$.

G The number of dark is half the number of milk.

H 75% of them are milk.

E Writing in the form $k:1$ and $1:k$ level 6

1 To make breakfast juice, orange and grapefruit juice are mixed in the ratio $4:3$.
How much grapefruit juice is needed to mix with 1 litre of orange juice?

2 Write each of these ratios in the form $k:1$.

(a) $5:2$ **(b)** $18:10$ **(c)** $420:350$ **(d)** $180:80$ **(e)** $6:10$

3 Write each of these ratios in the form $1:k$.

(a) $2:7$ **(b)** $5:12$ **(c)** $4:10$ **(d)** $10:9$ **(e)** $5:4$

4 In a swimming club there are 16 boys and 20 girls.
Write the ratio boys:girls in the form $1:k$.

5 A business card is 9 cm wide and 5 cm high.
Write the ratio width:height in the form $k:1$.

19 Substitution

A Substitution review

 1 Work out the values of these expressions when $p = 3$.

(a) $4p^2$

(b) $7(p + 3)$

(c) $20 - 3p$

(d) $\dfrac{150}{5p}$

(e) $4(p - 8)$

(f) $\dfrac{2p^2}{3}$

(g) $15 - p^2$

(h) $5 - p^2$

(i) $\dfrac{7}{p - 2}$

(j) $\dfrac{108}{p^2}$

(k) $150 - 2p^2$

(l) $\dfrac{3 - 5p^2}{2}$

2 The cost £C of hiring a car for the day and driving d miles is given by the formula $C = 20 + 0.3d$.

How much will it cost to hire the car and drive 69 miles?

3 Work out the value of each of these.

(a) $1.2h + 4$ when $h = 1.6$

(b) $6a^2 + a$ when $a = 2.3$

(c) $\dfrac{14}{5n - 10.2}$ when $n = 2.6$

(d) $2.5b^2 - 3b$ when $b = 3.6$

(e) $1.6e(5e + 1.2)$ when $e = 5.2$

(f) $\dfrac{h^2}{7} + 3.5h$ when $h = 4.2$

B Expressions with more than one letter

1 Calculate the value of each of these when $a = 3$, $b = 4$ and $c = 6$.

(a) $b(c - a)$

(b) $a^2 + b^2$

(c) $(a + b)^2$

(d) $\dfrac{bc}{a}$

(e) $2c - 3a$

(f) $\dfrac{c}{b + 2}$

(g) $\dfrac{c}{ab}$

(h) $2ab - c$

2 Calculate the value of each of these when $a = {}^-2$, $b = 4$ and $c = 5$.

(a) $a(b + c)$

(b) $ab + c$

(c) $\dfrac{bc}{a}$

(d) $3b^2$

(e) $\dfrac{b + c}{a}$

(f) $2b^2 + 3c^2$

(g) $a^2 + b^2 + c^2$

(h) $c^2 - b^2$

3 Given that $a = 2$ and $b = 5$, calculate the value of each of these.

(a) ab^2

(b) a^2b

(c) $(a + b)^2$

(d) a^2b^2

4 Evaluate each of these when $a = \frac{1}{5}$, $b = \frac{1}{4}$ and $c = \frac{3}{10}$.

(a) $3b$

(b) $3a - c$

(c) $a + b$

(d) $a + b + c$

(e) $a + b - c$

5 Given that $a = 4.2$, $b = 3.6$ and $c = 9.2$, evaluate each of these expressions, giving answers correct to two decimal places.

(a) $\dfrac{a}{c - b}$ (b) $\dfrac{ab}{c}$ (c) $c - \dfrac{a}{b}$ (d) $3b^2$

(e) ac^2 (f) $\dfrac{b + c}{a + b}$ (g) $ac + ba$ (h) $\dfrac{b^2 + 1}{3a}$

6 Evaluate each of these expressions when $a = 3.5$, $b = {}^-2.5$ and $c = {}^-0.5$.

(a) $\dfrac{a^2}{b^2}$ (b) $(a - 3b)^2$ (c) $4a^2$ (d) $(4a)^2$

(e) $ab + bc + ca$ (f) $1.2a - 3.5b$ (g) $(2a + b)^2$ (h) $b^2 - c^2$

c Units in formulas

1 The formula to find the perimeter of a rectangle is $p = 2(l + w)$ where l is the length and w is the width of the rectangle.

Use the formula to calculate the perimeters of rectangles with these dimensions. Remember to include the units in your answers.

(a) $l = 5\,\text{m}$, $w = 70\,\text{cm}$ (b) $l = 18\,\text{mm}$, $w = 2\,\text{cm}$

2 The area of a triangle is given by the formula $A = \frac{1}{2}bh$.

The area of a trapezium is given by the formula $A = \frac{1}{2}(a + b)h$.

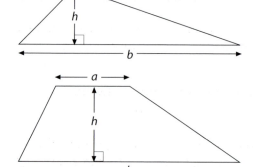

(a) Calculate the areas of these shapes. Each one is a triangle or a trapezium.

(i) 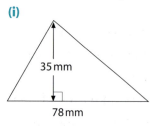   (ii) 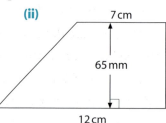   (iii)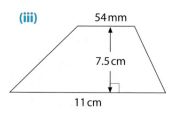

(b) Calculate the area of a triangle for which $b = 11.6\,\text{cm}$ and $h = 23\,\text{mm}$.

(c) Calculate the area of a trapezium for which $a = 2.5\,\text{m}$, $b = 4\,\text{m}$ and $h = 34\,\text{cm}$.

3 The surface area of a cube is given by the formula $s = 6l^2$
where l is the length of an edge.

Calculate the surface area of cubes with these edge lengths.

(a) 3 cm   **(b)** 4.5 m   **(c)** 6.8 mm

4 The surface area of a cuboid is given by the formula $s = 2bw + 2bl + 2lw$
where b, l and w are the lengths of the edges.

Calculate the surface area of this cuboid.

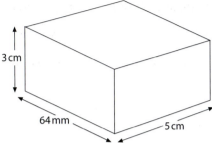

3 cm

64 mm

5 cm

D Mixed questions

1 An approximate formula to calculate the stopping distance m, in metres, for a car
travelling at a speed of k kilometres per hour is $m = 0.006k^2 + 0.19k$.

Use the formula to estimate the stopping distance for a car travelling at 40 km per hour.

2 The lowest temperature possible is 0 K on the Kelvin scale or $^-$273 °C in degrees Celsius.
The formula to convert from temperature in °C (C) to temperature in Kelvin (K) is

$$K = C + 273$$

Convert these temperatures to Kelvin.

(a) 30 °C   **(b)** 0 °C   **(c)** $^-$20 °C   **(d)** $^-$250 °C

3 The mass of a piece of wood is given by the formula $M = 0.7V$
where M is the mass of the wood in grams and V is the volume of the wood in cm³.

(a) Find the mass of a piece of wood that has a volume of 500 cm³.

(b) Work out the mass in kilograms of a block of wood that has a volume of 5600 cm³.

4 As you go up a mountain the temperature drops.

The amount by which the temperature drops is given roughly by the formula $t = \dfrac{m}{200}$.

t is the drop in temperature in °C and m is the height above sea level in metres.

The peak of Mount Everest is almost 9 km above sea level.

(a) Work out the rough drop in temperature from sea level to the top of Everest.

(b) **(i)** If the temperature at sea level is 15 °C, about what is the temperature
at the top of Everest?

    (ii) Use the formula $F = \dfrac{9C}{5} + 32$ to convert this temperature to °F.

20 Scaling and ratio

A Scaling drawings
B Scaling down

1 Measure the lengths of all the sides of this original shape and the scaled copy of it.

What scale factor has been used to make the copy?

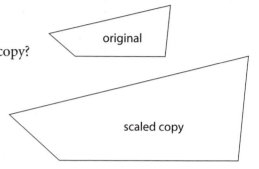

original

scaled copy

2 Ramni uses this table to make a scale drawing of a bird box.

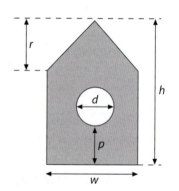

	Length on real bird box	Length on scale drawing
Height of box (*h*)	24 cm	4.8 cm
Width of box (*w*)	15 cm	
Diameter of hole (*d*)		1.2 cm
Height of roof (*r*)	9 cm	
Position of hole (*p*)		1.4 cm

(a) What scale factor has he used to get lengths for the scale drawing?

(b) Copy the table and fill in the missing numbers.

3 Measure the sides next to the right angle in each of these right-angled triangles.

Which triangles are enlargements of triangle A? Give the scale factor for those that are.

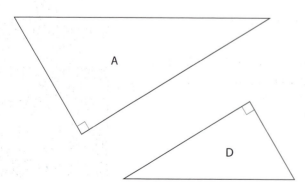

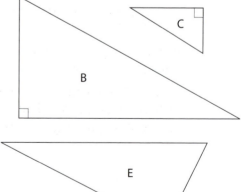

c Proportion within a shape

1 Find the ratio $\dfrac{\text{longest side}}{\text{shortest side}}$ for each of these rectangles.

Use these ratios to find pairs where one rectangle is an enlargement of the other.

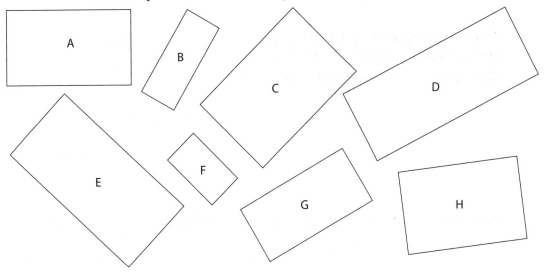

2 (a) Calculate the ratio $\dfrac{\text{width}}{\text{height}}$ for this rectangle.

(b) A copy of this rectangle has height 5.2 cm. Calculate its width.

(c) Another rectangle has height 4.0 cm and width 4.9 cm. State whether it is a copy of the rectangle shown here, giving your reasons.

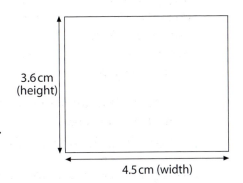

3.6 cm (height)

4.5 cm (width)

3 (a) An enlargement of this photo has a height of 21.0 cm. Calculate its width.

(b) A smaller copy of the photo has a width of 5.0 cm. Calculate its height.

(c) A photo has a height of 38.5 cm and a width of 28.0 cm. State whether it is the right size to be an enlargement of this photograph, giving your reasons.

8.0 cm

11.0 cm

21 Understanding inequalities

A Single inequalities

1 Decide whether each of these is true or false.

(a) $^-3 < ^-5$ (b) $0 \leq ^-3$ (c) $0.39 \leq 0.4$

(d) $0.22 > 0.2$ (e) $\sqrt{12} \leq 3$ (f) $0.09 > 0.1$

(g) $\frac{1}{5} < \frac{1}{3}$ (h) $(^-3)^2 < 3$ (i) $\frac{1}{5} < 0.2$

2 (a) For the set of values $x \leq 3$, which of the numbers in the loop are values of x?

(b) Which are values of p for the set $p > 7$?

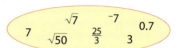
$\sqrt{7}$ $^-7$ 0.7   7 $\sqrt{50}$ $\frac{25}{3}$ 3

3 Write an inequality for each of these diagrams.

(a)
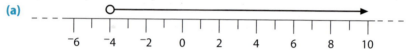

(b)
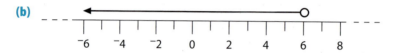

(c)
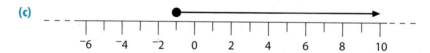

4 For each of these, sketch a number line and draw the inequality on it.

(a) $p \geq ^-2$ (b) $x > 5$ (c) $x \leq 3\frac{1}{2}$

5 (a) Find three pairs of equivalent inequalities.

| $7 \geq n$ | $7 > n$ | $n < 7$ | $7 < n$ | $n \leq 7$ | $n > 7$ |

(b) Sketch a number line and draw the inequality $^-1 > x$ on it.

*6 Given that $x < 7$, decide whether each of these is always true, sometimes true or never true.

(a) $x < 9$ (b) $x > 5$ (c) $\frac{x}{2} < 8$

(d) $2x > 14$ (e) $x + 3 < 10$ (f) $x + 4 > 12$

B Combined inequalities

1 Sketch a number line to represent each inequality.

   (a) $3 < x \le 7$ **(b)** $^-4 \le x < 5$ **(c)** $^-2 \le x \le 4$

2 (a) Which of the numbers in the loop are in
the set of values of x given by $^-1 \le x < 3$?

   (b) Which are in the set of values of n
given by $^-8 \le n \le 1$?

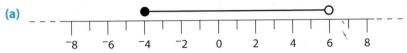
$$0 \qquad \sqrt{8} \quad \tfrac{3}{2} \quad ^-1 \quad ^-9$$
$$^-0.5 \qquad ^-6 \quad 3$$

3 Write an inequality for each of these diagrams.

   (a)

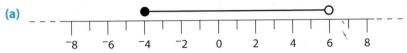

   (b)

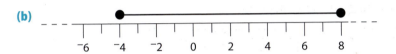

   (c)

4 List five different values of n that satisfy $^-3 < n \le 1$.

5 Integers are positive and negative whole numbers including zero.
Find all the integers p so that $p^2 < 15$.

6 Find two integers n so that $14 < n^2 < 30$.

7 List four different integers x so that $^-3 \le 3x \le 12$.

C Converting between words and symbols

1 Write each of these as a mathematical statement.
   (a) The theatre will hold up to 500 people. (Use p for the number of people.)
   (b) I ate at least eight red sweets. (Use s for the number of sweets eaten.)
   (c) Store at a temperature less than 50 °C. (Use t to stand for the temperature.)
   (d) I will not sell my car for less than £4000. (Use s for the selling price.)

2 Make up a statement for each of these inequalities.
State what each letter stands for.
   (a) $p > 10$ **(b)** $t \le 32$ **(c)** $n < 100$

22 Sequences

A Sequences from shapes

1 From this loop, write down all the

  (a) odd numbers

  (b) square numbers

  (c) triangle numbers

  (d) cube numbers

1   8 9 12 15   27 30 40 64

2 Find

  (a) the 12th square number   (b) the 4th triangle number

  (c) the 5th cube number   (d) the 1000th even number

  (e) the 50th odd number   (f) all the odd triangle numbers less than 30

B Continuing linear sequences

1 (a) Find the next two terms in each sequence.

    (i) 6, 10, 14, 18, 22, … , …   (ii) 3, 6, 12, 24, … , …

    (iii) 3, 8, 13, 18, 23, … , …   (iv) 10, 8, 6, 4, 2, … , …

  (b) Which of the sequences in part (a) are linear?

2 A sequence of numbers begins 36, 20, 12, 8, …
The rule for this sequence is 'add 4 to the last term then halve the result'.

  (a) Find the next three terms.   (b) Is the sequence linear?

3 A sequence of numbers begins 2, 3, 5, 8, 12, 17, …

  (a) What are the next two terms?

  (b) Describe a rule to go from one term to the next.

  (c) Is the sequence linear?

4 Find the next three terms in the sequence 3, 5, 9, 15, 23, …

5 The first four terms of a linear sequence are 7, 9, 11, 13, …
Explain how you can work out the 50th term of this sequence.

6 Each sequence below is linear.
Copy each sequence and fill in the missing numbers.

  (a) 4, 9, __ , __ , __ , 29, …   (b) 30, __ , 22, __ , 14, 10, …

  (c) 1, __ , 13, __ , 25, __ , …   (d) __ , 17, __ , __ , 23, __ , …

C The *n*th term

1 The *n*th term of a sequence is $6n - 1$.

   (a) Write down the first five terms of the sequence.

   (b) Calculate the 20th term.

2 The *n*th term of a sequence is $5n + 4$.
Find the 100th term in this sequence.

3 A sequence begins $7, 5, 3, 1, ^-1, \ldots$

   (a) Which of these is its *n*th term?
      $2n + 5$ $5 - 2n$ $9 - 2n$

   (b) Write down its tenth term.

4 The *n*th terms of six different sequences are

 $n + 2$ **B** $3 - n$ **C** n^2 **D** $\frac{1}{2}n$ **E** $2n + 1$ **F** $\dfrac{120}{n}$

   (a) Calculate the first five terms of each sequence.

   (b) Which of these sequences are linear?

D The *n*th term of a linear sequence
E The *n*th term of other sequences

1 A sequence begins $2, 5, 8, 11, 14, \ldots$

   (a) What is the 10th term?

   (b) Sam says the *n*th term of this sequence is $n + 3$.
Sam is wrong.
What is the *n*th term of this sequence?

> It goes up in 3s so it's $n + 3$.

2 For each of the following sequences

     • find an expression for the *n*th term

     • use your expression to work out the 20th term

   (a) $6, 10, 14, 18, 22, \ldots$ **(b)** $11, 21, 31, 41, 51, \ldots$ **(c)** $5, 8, 11, 14, 17, \ldots$

   (d) $1, 4, 7, 10, 13, \ldots$ **(e)** $11, 20, 29, 38, 47, \ldots$ **(e)** $3, 11, 19, 27, 35, \ldots$

3 A sequence begins $20, 18, 16, 14, 12, \ldots$

   (a) What are the next two terms?   **(b)** What is the *n*th term?

4 For each of the following sequences find the *n*th term.

   (a) $50, 48, 46, 44, 42, \ldots$ **(b)** $17, 14, 11, 8, 5, \ldots$

   (c) $22, 16, 10, 4, ^-2, \ldots$ **(d)** $2, ^-1, ^-4, ^-7, ^-10, \ldots$

5 **A**   4, 7, 12, 19, 28, …   **B**   2, 7, 12, 17, 22, …   **C**   10, 40, 90, 160, 250, …

(a) Which of these sequences is a linear sequence?

(b) What is the next term in each sequence?

(c) Find the nth term of each sequence.

F Ways of seeing

G Ways of seeing further

1 A pattern is made with sticks.

Pattern 1   Pattern 2   Pattern 3
8 sticks   15 sticks   22 sticks

(a) (i) Draw a diagram to show pattern 4.

    (ii) How many sticks are there in pattern 4?

(b) How many sticks are there in pattern 10?

(c) Find a rule for the number of sticks in pattern n.
Explain how you found your rule.

(d) How many sticks would you need for pattern 100?

2 Jigsaw puzzles have

  and

(a) This is a 5 by 5 square jigsaw.

    (i) How many corner pieces are there?

    (ii) How many edge pieces are there?

    (iii) How many middle pieces are there?

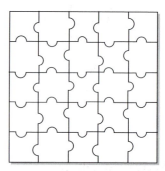

(b) How many edge pieces are there in an 8 by 8 square jigsaw?

(c) How many middle pieces are there in a 12 by 12 square jigsaw?

(d) For an n by n square jigsaw, find a rule for the number of

    (i) corner pieces   (ii) edge pieces   (iii) middle pieces

3 Pearlystrings make necklaces and pendants from tiny pearls strung on thread.
These are some of their designs.

For each necklace design

    (i)   draw pattern 4 and write down how many pearls are used

    (ii) find how many pearls are used in pattern 5 and pattern 10

    (iii) find a rule for the number of pearls in the nth pattern

(a) Necklace design A

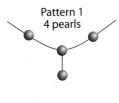
Pattern 1
4 pearls

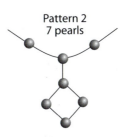
Pattern 2
7 pearls

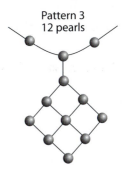
Pattern 3
12 pearls

(b) Necklace design B

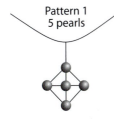
Pattern 1
5 pearls

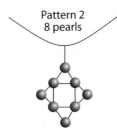
Pattern 2
8 pearls

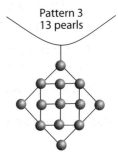
Pattern 3
13 pearls

(c) Necklace design C

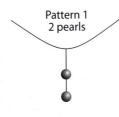
Pattern 1
2 pearls

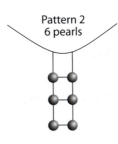
Pattern 2
6 pearls

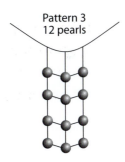
Pattern 3
12 pearls

*(d) Necklace design D

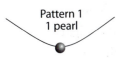
Pattern 1
1 pearl

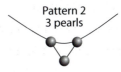
Pattern 2
3 pearls

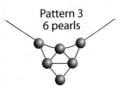
Pattern 3
6 pearls

23 Paired data

You need graph paper.

A Scatter diagrams and correlation

level 6

1 The table below shows the cost in £ of nine different makes of battery and the lifetime of each of them in hours.

Battery	A	B	C	D	E	F	G	H	I
Cost (£)	1.35	0.95	0.70	1.10	0.65	1.50	1.75	0.60	1.20
Lifetime (hours)	15	12	8	15	10	16	17	11	11

(a) Draw a scatter diagram for this data with cost across and lifetime up.

(b) Describe the correlation between cost and lifetime.

2 The 'Modern Pentathlon' event in the Olympic Games consists of five contests: shooting, swimming, fencing, equestrian and running.
The table below shows the points scored by the top ten competitors in the 2004 men's pentathlon in shooting and swimming.

Competitor	A	B	C	D	E	F	G	H	I	J
Shooting	1036	1000	1084	1096	1168	1108	952	1036	988	1156
Swimming	1376	1308	1336	1252	1332	1260	1336	1240	1252	1216

(a) Draw a scatter diagram for this data with scales labelled as follows.
Across: from 900 to 1200   Up: from 1200 to 1400

(b) Describe the correlation between the two scores.

(c) Would it be possible to predict a competitor's swimming score from their shooting score?

B Line of best fit
C Interpreting scatter diagrams

1 The table gives the neck girth (in cm) and the mass (in kg) of nine bears captured in a wildlife reserve.

Neck girth (cm)	35	39	40	46	36	50	48	40	43
Mass (kg)	23	38	43	61	24	77	69	41	52

(a) Draw a scatter diagram to show this information.

(b) Draw a line of best fit.

(c) Use the line to estimate the mass of a bear whose neck girth is 44 cm.

2 Ten cars of the same model are offered for sale in a local paper. The table below shows the age, mileage and price of each car. ('61k' means 61 000.)

Car	A	B	C	D	E	F	G	H	I	J
Age (years)	5	2	3	5	7	4	6	3	6	8
Mileage	61k	30k	42k	58k	69k	50k	63k	39k	64k	80k
Price (£)	3600	6000	5000	3800	2500	4200	3100	5300	2900	1900

(a) (i) Draw a scatter diagram for age and price.

   (ii) Draw a line of best fit.

(b) (i) Draw a scatter diagram for mileage and price.

   (ii) Draw a line of best fit.

(c) A car of this model is 4 years old with a mileage of 55k.

   (i) Use the first line of best fit to estimate a price for the car.

   (ii) Now use the second line of best fit to estimate a price.

   (iii) What price do you suggest that the car should be offered for?

(d) Would it be sensible to use the second line of best fit to estimate the price of a car with a mileage of 100k? Explain your answer.

3 The scatter diagram below shows the average speed of the Olympic record holders in the men's 100 m, 200 m, 400 m, 800 m, 1500 m and 5000 m races.

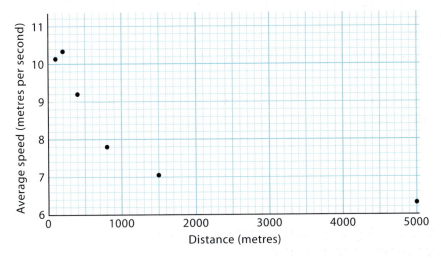

(a) Explain why it would not be sensible to draw a line of best fit in this case.

(b) (i) From the diagram estimate roughly the record average speed in metres per second for a 1000 metre race.

   (ii) Use your estimate to calculate an estimate of the record time for a 1000 metre race.

24 Working with coordinates

You need centimetre squared paper.

A Shapes on a coordinate grid	level 6
B Mid-point of a line segment	level 6

1 Which of the points W, X, Y and Z can be
joined to A and C to give

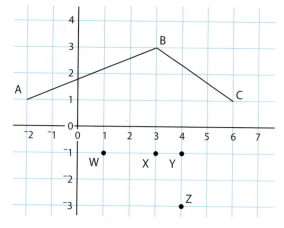

   (a) a kite

   (b) a parallelogram

   (c) a trapezium

2 Write down the coordinates of the fourth vertex of each of these quadrilaterals.

   (a) A rectangle with vertices at (⁻2, 5), (⁻5, 2), (1, ⁻4)

   (b) A parallelogram with vertices at (3, 3), (⁻2, 3) and (⁻4, ⁻1)

   (c) A kite with vertices at (2, 6), (⁻1, 4) and (2, ⁻2)

3 What are the mid-points of the line segments joining these pairs of points?

   (a) (2, 0) and (4, 10)   **(b)** (3, ⁻1) and (5, 5)   **(c)** (2, ⁻2) and (⁻1, 6)

4 (a) On a one-centimetre coordinate grid, plot the points P (⁻2, 2), Q (2, 4),
      R (10, 2) and S (2, ⁻2) and join them to make a quadrilateral.

   (b) (i) What can you say about the line segments PQ and SR?

      (ii) What is the special name for quadrilateral PQRS?

   (c) Work out the area of PQRS.

   (d) (i) Mark the mid-point of each edge of PQRS.
        Join the mid-points up to form a new quadrilateral.

      (ii) Write down the special name for the new quadrilateral.

      (iii) How are the areas of PQRS and the new quadrilateral related?

5 Point A (⁻2, ⁻1) is one end of a line segment AB.
The mid-point of the line segment is (2, 2).
What are the coordinates of point B?

In each question, the coordinates refer to a square centimetre grid.

1 Calculate the lengths of line segments with these end points.

(a) $(1, 2)$ and $(4, ^-2)$ (b) $(3, 4)$ and $(^-2, 2)$ (c) $(6, 1)$ and $(^-1, ^-3)$

2 A quadrilateral has vertices at A $(1, 1)$, B $(1, 4)$, C $(4, 4)$ and D $(7, ^-1)$.

(a) Find the length of each edge.

(b) Explain how you know that the shape is not a kite.

3 PQRS a rhombus, with P at $(1, 6)$ and Q at $(8, 7)$.
The diagonals of the rhombus cross at $(2, 4)$.

(a) Give the coordinates of R and S.

(b) Find the area of the rhombus.

4 (a) On a coordinate grid, plot and join the points P $(^-7, 1)$, Q $(^-2, 6)$, R $(4, 4)$ and S $(5, ^-3)$ to make a quadrilateral.

(b) What can you say about the line segments QR and PS?

(c) Calculate the lengths of PQ and RS.

(d) What kind of quadrilateral have you drawn?

(e) Draw in any lines of symmetry.

5 (a) On a pair of axes, each numbered from $^-6$ to 10, draw the lines with equations $y = 2x + 7$ and $x + y = 10$.

(b) What are the coordinates of the point where the lines cross?
Label this point K.

KLMN is a parallelogram.
The diagonals of the parallelogram cross at the point $(2, 5)$.
L is a point on the line $x + y = 10$.
N is a point on the line $y = 2x + 7$.

(c) Draw the parallelogram and give the coordinates of points L, M and N.

(d) Describe fully any rotation symmetry in the parallelogram KLMN.

6 ABCD is a kite.
A and B are points on the line $y = 2x - 2$.
B and C are points on the line $y = 10 - 2x$.
Point D has coordinates $(^-5, 4)$.
The area of the kite is $32 \, cm^2$.

(a) Draw the kite in the correct position on a coordinate grid.

(b) Find the equation of the line of symmetry.

(c) What type of quadrilateral is made by joining the mid-points of the edges?

25 Brackets and equations

1 Simplify these expressions.

(a) $(a + 1) + (5a - 3)$

(b) $(4 - a) + (8a - 1)$

(c) $(9a - 5) + (8 - 3a)$

(d) $(5 - 2p) + (7 - 3p)$

(e) $5p - (4p + 2)$

(f) $(4p + 6) - (3p + 2)$

(g) $(6x + 5) - (x - 2)$

(h) $(6 - 2x) - (4x + 2)$

(i) $(9 - x) - (3 - 4x)$

(j) $(6 - y) - (3 + 4y)$

(k) $(7 - 2y) - (6 - y)$

(l) $(y + 8) - (10y + 1)$

2 Simplify these expressions.

(a) $9a + 4(2 + a)$

(b) $5(a - 4) + 2(3a - 2)$

(c) $8(a + 5) + 3(3 - a)$

(d) $7n - 3(n + 4)$

(e) $7(2n + 3) - 6(3 + n)$

(f) $5(3n + 4) - 4(n - 3)$

(g) $5(x - 5) - 4(1 + x)$

(h) $12x - 5(2x - 3)$

(i) $4(x + 4) - 2(8 - 3x)$

3 Simplify these expressions.

(a) $12 + \dfrac{18x + 21}{3}$

(b) $\frac{1}{2}(6y + 8) + 3(4 + y)$

(c) $\dfrac{4z + 2}{2} + 3(2 - z)$

(d) $\dfrac{24a + 12}{3} - 5(a + 2)$

(e) $\dfrac{16b + 8}{4} - 2(4 - b)$

(f) $\dfrac{24c + 18}{6} - 3(c - 5)$

C Simplifying to solve an equation

1 (a) Simplify the expression $3n + 7(n - 3)$.

(b) Use the result of part (a) to solve the equation $3n + 7(n - 3) = 19$.

2 (a) Simplify the expression $5x - 3(x - 9)$.

(b) Use the result of part (a) to solve the equation $5x - 3(x - 9) = 21$.

3 Solve these equations.

(a) $12 + 3(x - 5) = 33$

(b) $5x - 4(x + 1) = 10$

(c) $x + 5(x - 2) = 5$

(d) $1 - 3(2x - 5) = 22$

(e) $5x - 3(2 - x) = 6$

(f) $2(4 - 3x) + 7(x + 2) = 19$

(g) $2(x + 5) - 3(1 - 2x) = 39$

(h) $3(2x + 9) - 4(1 - x) = 3$

4 Solve these equations.

(a) $8 - (2 + n) = n + 5$

(b) $4n + 3(3 + n) = 2n + 19$

(c) $8n - 2(2n - 5) = 7(n - 2)$

(d) $5(n - 1) - 3(1 - 4n) = 2(n + 11)$

26 Roots

A Squares and cubes
B Square and cube roots

level 6

1 Evaluate these.

(a) 10 squared
(b) The cube of 3
(c) 5 cubed
(d) The square of 12

2 Evaluate these.

(a) 4^2
(b) $(^-3)^2$
(c) 4^3
(d) $(^-4)^3$
(e) $(^-5)^2$

3 Find the positive and negative square roots of these.

(a) 81
(b) 100
(c) 49
(d) 144
(e) 1

4 Find the cube root of these.

(a) 27
(b) $^-8$
(c) 64
(d) $^-1$
(e) 125

5 Solve these equations.

(a) $p^3 = 1000$
(b) $q^2 + 18 = 82$
(c) $5r^2 = 45$
(d) $\dfrac{s^3}{3} = 72$

*6 (a) These digit cards can be arranged to make two square numbers. What are the two square numbers?

5 2 6

(b) Find three digit cards that can be arranged to make **three** different square numbers, each with three digits.

D Cube roots on a calculator

1 Evaluate these, correct to 2 d.p.

(a) $\sqrt[3]{200}$
(b) $\sqrt[3]{-184}$
(c) $\sqrt[3]{45 + 32}$
(d) $\sqrt[3]{\dfrac{15}{4}}$

(e) $\sqrt[3]{25.6} + \sqrt{10.3}$
(f) $\sqrt[3]{\dfrac{8.9^2}{7.5}}$
(g) $\dfrac{\sqrt[3]{8.67 - 4.13}}{1.34}$
(h) $\sqrt[3]{\dfrac{49.2 + 36.1}{51.8 - 24.6}}$

2 A tin is in the shape of a cylinder, with its height equal to its radius. A formula to find the radius of the cylinder is

$$r = \sqrt[3]{\dfrac{V}{\pi}}$$

where r is the radius and V is the volume of the cylinder.

(a) When $V = 250$, what is the value of r correct to 2 d.p?

(b) If the tin has a volume of $400 \, cm^3$, what is the radius of the tin? Give your answer correct to 2 d.p.

Mixed practice 3

You need graph paper.

1 A cake recipe uses 125 g of butter and 200 g of sugar.
Write the ratio of butter to sugar in its simplest form.

2 The nth term of a sequence is given by the expression $n^2 + 20$.
Work out the 7th term of the sequence.

3 (a) Draw a pair of axes, each numbered from $^-4$ to 6.
Plot the points P $(^-2, 0)$, Q $(0, 4)$ and R $(6, 1)$.

   (b) (i) Plot the point S so that PQRS is a rectangle.

       (ii) What are the coordinates of S?

   (c) Draw all the lines of symmetry on the rectangle.

4 Find the cube root of 1 million.

5 The table shows the lengths and widths of some leaves on a shrub.

Length (mm)	130	123	112	142	126	115	113	136	134	103
Width (mm)	52	46	44	58	49	49	47	50	53	40

   (a) Show this information on a scatter diagram.

   (b) Draw the line of best fit on your scatter diagram.

   (c) Use your graph to estimate the width of a leaf with length 120 mm.

   (d) If you used the graph to estimate the width of a leaf that is 150 mm long,
would you expect your answer to be accurate?

6 At ground level, water boils at 100 °C.
As you go up a mountain, the boiling point is given by the rule $b = 100 - \dfrac{h}{1000}$
where b is the boiling point in °C and h is the height in feet.
Mount McKinley in Alaska is about 20 000 feet high.
What is the boiling point of water on top of Mount McKinley?

7 What is the largest three-digit square number?

8 Simplify each expression.

   (a) $2(n + 3) + \dfrac{6n - 15}{3}$ **(b)** $6n - (2 - 3n)$ **(c)** $10n - 3(2n + 1)$

9 The mid-point of a line segment AB is $\left(1\tfrac{1}{2}, 5\right)$.
Point A has coordinates $(4, ^-1)$.
Find the coordinates of point B.

10 Find an expression for the nth term of the sequence 5, 12, 19, 26, 33, 40, …

11 Decide whether each of these statements is true or false.

(a) $\frac{3}{10} > 0.25$　　(b) $\pi < 3$　　(c) $0.2^2 > 0.1$　　(d) $\frac{1}{4} > \left(\frac{1}{2}\right)^2$

12 Lilac gold is made from gold and zinc in the ratio $3:1$.

(a) What weight of lilac gold can be made with 24 grams of gold?

(b) How much zinc is needed to make 40 grams of lilac gold?

13 Work out the value of each of these expressions when $a = 3$ and $b = {}^-5$.

(a) $4a^2 + a$　　(b) $5a + 2b$　　(c) $2ab$　　(d) $\dfrac{a - b}{a + b}$　　(e) $(a + b)^2$

14 (a) Find two square numbers s such that $50 < s < 100$.

(b) Find all the prime numbers p that satisfy $5 \leq p \leq 25$.

15 A designer has a photograph 136 mm wide by 208 mm high.
She wants to reduce it so its width is 102 mm to fit in a column of a magazine.

(a) What scale factor should she use?

(b) How high will the picture be when it is printed in the magazine?

16 A school has a box containing 2350 centimetre cubes.
What are the dimensions of the largest solid cube that can be made from these cubes?

17 Sketch a number line to represent the inequality ${}^-3 \leq n < 2$.

18 A sequence of numbers begins 5, 16, 49, 148, 445, …

(a) Describe a rule to go from one term to the next.

(b) Using your rule, find the next term.

(c) Is the sequence linear?

19 To make a fruit drink Leo mixes orange, lemon and pineapple juice in the ratio $8:3:4$.

(a) How many millilitres of pineapple juice does he need to make 3 litres of the drink?

(b) What percentage of the drink is lemon juice?

20 These patterns are made with counters.

pattern 1

pattern 2

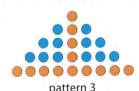
pattern 3

(a) How many orange counters will there be in pattern 4?

(b) Find an expression for the number of orange counters in pattern n.
Explain how you found your expression.

(c) Find an expression for the number of blue counters in pattern n.

21 Write the ratio 2 kg : 250 g in its simplest form.

22 A stone is projected up so that its height, h metres above the ground, after t seconds is given by $h = 20t - 5t^2$.

    (a) Show that the stone is 8.75 metres above the ground after 0.5 seconds.

    (b) How far from the ground is the stone after 3.9 seconds?

23 Show that B is not a scaled copy of A.

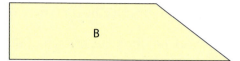

24 Evaluate each of these expressions when $a = {}^-1.3$, $b = 5.9$ and $c = {}^-0.7$. Give each result correct to two decimal places.

    (a) a^2b **(b)** ab^2 **(c)** $\dfrac{a}{b+c}$ **(d)** $ab - bc$ **(e)** $\dfrac{a^2}{b^2 - c^2}$

25 Evaluate $\sqrt[3]{2.5^2 - 1.9^2}$ correct to three significant figures.

26 Given that $r = \frac{3}{5}$ and $t = \frac{2}{3}$, find the value of

    (a) $r + t$ **(b)** $4t$ **(c)** rt **(d)** $r \div 3$ **(e)** t^2

27 Solve these equations.

    (a) $x^2 = 25$ **(b)** $6p^2 = 54$ **(c)** $z^3 = 8$ **(d)** $5t^3 = {}^-320$

28 These patterns are made with counters.

    (a) How many yellow counters will there be in pattern 5?

    (b) What is an expression for the number of yellow counters in pattern n? Explain how you found your expression.

pattern 1   pattern 2   pattern 3   pattern 4

29 Solve these equations.

    (a) $6n - 2(n + 3) = 12$ **(b)** $3(k + 1) + 4(2k - 3) = 24$ **(c)** $2(2x + 1) - (6 - x) = 7x$

30 **(a)** Draw a pair of axes, each numbered from ${}^-6$ to 8. Plot the points $A\,({}^-1, 8)$, $B\,(7, 4)$ and $C\,(3, {}^-4)$.

    (b) **(i)** Plot the point D so that ABCD is a square.

         (ii) What are the coordinates of D?

    (c) Plot and join the mid-points of each side of ABCD.

    (d) Calculate the ratio $\dfrac{\text{side length of larger square}}{\text{side length of smaller square}}$, correct to 3 d.p.

*31 A landowner divides the area of her land between orchards and fields in the ratio $6:1$. The orchard area is divided between apples and plums in the ratio $2:1$. What fraction of the total area of land is apple orchards?